DISCOVER YOU DISCOVERING THE WORLD
Confessions of A Traveling Monkette

Laura Louise Persichetti

Discover You Discovering the World
Confessions of A Traveling Monkette

Published By Laura Louise Inspires
ISBN 978-1484806807

Book Design
By Milton Howard, Jr.
www.hdlife.org

Art Design
By Ryan Schwartz
www.ryan-schwartz.com

Photography
By Robert Rondinelli
www.rlrphotography.com

www.discoveryoubook.com
www.liveandlovewithlaura.com

Dedication

Dedicated to those who have contemplated suicide.

Although anyone may find the practices, strategies, stories, and exercises in this book to be useful, it is sold with the understanding that the author is not engaged in presenting specific medical, psychological or emotional advice. Each person has unique needs and this book cannot take individual differences into account. Anyone who is suffering from suicidal thoughts, depression, stress, anxiety or any emotional, physical and/or spiritual distress is encouraged to seek support outside of this book, consult with a medical doctor or licensed therapist to support you in your own personal growth.

Acknowledgments

I grew up watching soap operas so the Day Time Emmy Awards were one of my favourite award shows to watch. On commercials I regularly stepped onto the brick level in front of our fireplace in the family room and with the remote in my hand as the microphone, I'd practice my thank you speech. I look forward to this year's Day Time Emmy's to practice once again, but for now, I will stick to the messages of gratitude, specific to the creation of this book:

A special thank you to Krystal Butler for being the first person to read these pages and for providing content and editing feedback. Her consistent support and loving care have always and continue to be most appreciated.

Thank you to Doug Allen for challenging me to write a book in two weeks and for the consistent support and challenges!

Thank you to Milton Howard for supporting the final creation of this book, creating the book cover, and for the loving encouragement: www.hdlife.org.

Thank you to Ryan Schwartz for his artistic talents on the cover image: www.ryan-schwartz.com

Thank you to Roberto Rondinelli for his photography on the back cover: www.rlrphotography.com

Thank you to my friends and family for providing me with the memories and experiences to develop content to write about. Special thanks to David!

Honourable mention to the special people who have passed: Great Aunt Sara, Uncle Lorenzo, Mrs. Van Hooren, Nadia, Noelle, Cameron, Remo Jesse, Beth, Nonnie, Rick, Ron T, Ron S, Mrs. McEwan, George, and Eugene.

Table of Contents

THE (HAPTER BEFORE THE (HAPTER

Read First!

I was going to call this the preface, but realized I never read a preface in a book before, so I couldn't assume that everyone who reads this book would also read a preface. So this is the chapter before the chapter. It is not a preface and it is not a forward, but essentially it is about moving forward. I have always wanted to be a writer. It was one of my greatest dreams, yet as much as I loved it, I wouldn't take the time to write. I would dream of myself living in a little cottage on the water, writing books and sharing my thoughts and ideas with the world. In reality, the only time I found myself writing was when I would travel. Other than some journaling, I would never take the time to write. Life happened and it didn't include me writing.

A good friend and mentor challenged me to write a book and he gave me a date. The challenge was to write the book in two weeks. So here it is. I did it. It was exciting and it was an accomplishment. However, afterwards, I took all kinds of time editing the book and looking into publishing books, and thinking about the cover or how to get it copyrighted. I debated in my head if I should hire a professional editor. I debated if I should self publish or print. Suddenly, I was stuck in my head. Being stuck in my head held me back from really moving forward with this idea of writing a book and getting it out there. Why did it matter if someone copied a message that just needed to get out? It really became a matter of trying to do it perfectly. Perfection. It became about the perfect grammar, perfect publishing, and perfect printing. Trying to be perfect. What a failure. Perfection is absolutely impossible, and in trying to be perfect, I was only holding myself back from just doing and being. The more time I took trying to be perfect, the more time I wasted. How often does that happen for all of us?

So I got over it. I decided that I didn't care about grammar, run on sentences, punctuation or even page numbers. No one was grading this book. This is my own project that wasn't being submitted to please anyone. If you want to know what page you are on, it's this page. Then it will be the next page. I recommend using a bookmark; however, I think book formatting will take care of that anyway. This is a book that just needed to get out there with the hope to make a difference. It is a written experience so people who read it can reflect on their journey called life and appreciate the lessons and gifts along the way. It will be the first of many. Hopefully, someone, somewhere will enjoy reading and taking something from it in order to grow. That's what life is about anyway, isn't it? If you are not growing, you are dying. I see only one option to aim for. Grow and live.

So read with an open mind, open eyes and an open heart. If you notice any grammatical errors, or you feel information was repeated, consider yourself mindful. Allow yourself to take that moment to re-read and soak in that particular message. Perhaps it is an error, or perhaps it is the divine grabbing your attention. You can decide for yourself. I might have just messed up on purpose to get your attention or repeated something that really needed to stick. It's really the message that matters, not the little details.

For additional love and support, check out Live and Love with Laura at:

www.liveandlovewithlaura.com

www.youtube.com/liveandlovewithlaura - Please Subscribe

www.facebook.com/liveandlovewithalura - LIKE the page

www.discoveryoubook.com
Receive additional videos related to the book

Join me on the journey to peace.

Thank you for allowing me to be part of your journey through this book. May the long time sun, shine upon you, all love surround you, and the pure light within you, guide you on.

Much love to you and safe travels.

THE LUGGAGE

I was four years old when I packed my first piece of luggage. I put all of my favourite things in a small gym bag. At the time this included my closest friends, which were some of my dearest stuffed animals. It also included my favourite green blanket, my baby blanket, that I slept with every night, my photo albums, my notebook, a box of markers, some of my favourite clothes, and a few of my favourite books. I kept this bag under my window. At night I would take out my stuffed animals and baby blanket to have with me in bed. During the day I might pull things out of the bag to use. However, I always returned everything to the bag and kept it under my window.

I would imagine my escape if the house ever burnt down. I knew if I heard the fire alarm go off, I was meant to crawl to my door and with the back of my hand touch the doorknob. If the doorknob was hot, I would know not to open the door because I would let smoke into my room from the fire. I knew if this were the case I would roll up clothes or blankets to put at the bottom of the door to keep the smoke from entering under it. I would always get nervous thinking about how to get out the window. I knew how to open the screen, but I didn't always unlatch it too easily. I would imagine if I were too nervous and could not open the screen successfully then I would have to take something to break my window. That was Plan B. In Plan A, I would imagine that opening the screen would be easy to do. In either plan, I would grab my gym bag and climb out onto the roof. It would be high and I would be so scared, but I knew, if I really had to, I could jump. I would think to myself that I would rather break my leg or arm than to stay in my room and burn to death.

This is a true story. I was four years old. I kept this bag under my window for years. Of course, as I got older some of the things in my little luggage would change, but it was always there. You know, just in case there was a fire. This sounds silly doesn't it? Also sounds like I could have had a high anxiety disorder, or perhaps Obsessive Compulsive Disorder. Someone may look at that and think that I died in a fire in a past life and I carried that fear over to this life. A child psychologist, I'm sure, could analyze this to pieces.

You want to know the truth? When I was in kindergarten I attended an assembly in the gym at my school. It was a presentation on fire safety. The presenters, which were puppets, acted out different scenarios to demonstrate what to do in case there was a fire. One thing they stressed was never to try to gather your things to take with you. The most important thing was to get out and get out fast. As a kid, I imagined all of my favourite things burning in a fire. That just could not happen. So that night I went home and I packed my first piece of luggage. I made sure all of my favourite things were together so in case of a fire, I could quickly grab it, throw it from the roof and jump.

Did I mention that I also hate puppets? Fires and puppets terrified me growing up. I had attachment issues to things as well. I was also scared that my parents were going to die. If a fire was in the hallway, my parents' window did not lead to a roof. It was open and very high. If someone were to jump from that window, I didn't think they would survive with a broken arm or leg. I would imagine myself getting out fast and I would be the first one out. I would run to the neighbor's house and make sure 911 knew they had to hurry up and save my parents. I knew my brother would be fine because he could always unlatch the screen with ease. At this point, I decided that it was my responsibility to save my family.

I'm not the only one that made big decisions like this at a young age. When we are infants we completely rely on someone else to meet our needs. That someone can be a parent or a family member, it can be a relative or a neighbor, a stranger or caregiver of some sort. Crying is the first way we learn to communicate. We cry when we need something and we hope that someone will be there to support us; sometimes there is and sometimes there is not.

We learn very early what we can expect from the world around us and we learn quite early what we need to do to get our needs met. For example, a child may cry and receive love and care right away. This child learns to speak up to have his/her need met. Another child may cry and cry and no one comes to offer love and care. That child may attempt to crawl on his own to find support. That same child may slip and hurt himself and then someone hears that the cry has changed to a painful cry and that is when a person responds. This child may learn that self-harm or pain will bring care and love. Another child may cry and cry and again, no one responds. That child may try to throw something and break something. Next a caregiver may respond, perhaps with care and love or perhaps with anger and frustration. At this point it doesn't matter to the child, someone responded and from this is born a person who uses negative behaviours to get attention. Lastly, a child may cry and cry and again, no one will come. This child will begin crawling to find support, and grab onto something to stand and begin walking. A caregiver enters the room and begins cheering and laughing, for it is the child's first steps; and here is born the over-achiever.

It sounds a little bit exaggerated doesn't it? But is it? We make a whole whack of seriously important decisions by the time we are five that tend to set up the world around us for the rest of our lives. Many would think this concept is entirely ridiculous, but most of these decisions are held in our subconscious mind. Most of these decisions make sense at the time, in the mind of a child. Look at my case, in just one example that I shared, I was scared of fire and puppets for most of my life and never really understood why. To this day, I am protective of my family and feel as though it is my responsibility to take care of them. Is this true? No, it's just what I created in my head and I did this at the age of four. It wasn't until I began reflecting on my life and developing an understanding that I carry around an invisible piece of luggage that can really be heavy and weigh me down at times. I began looking to my experiences and relationships, and my thoughts and beliefs about things in my life. I examined where all of those things came from. I wondered if I have been using these subconscious beliefs to empower myself or if I have been using them to weigh me down, holding me back. I started working through this invisible piece of luggage I had no idea I was carrying with me.

When we are children we decide whether we are good enough or not or what we need to do to receive love. We use helpful and unhelpful ways to cope, to communicate and to work through challenges. I watched one presentation with puppets and I decided I hated puppets. I decided that I needed to fear my house burning down. I decided I needed to take care of my family. I decided I needed to save all of my favourite things. These decisions developed my attachment issue. It is likely the reason I have boxes of things that I keep for 'memories'. I had trouble sleeping as a child; likely because I went to bed worried and concerned. No one knew any of this. I'm sure if my mother knew, I would have visited a counselor. I carried all of this in me and had no idea that I did until I started self-reflecting on my life, exploring my subconscious mind and exploring how I came to be the person that I grew up to be. That assembly is just one experience, one example that I have shared. Each experience we have, we decide what that experience means to us and that unfolds our perceptions, beliefs, and thoughts that we may or may not be aware of. This starts in our childhood and continues through life.

I also didn't talk for the first three years of my life. My Nonna thought I had a hearing problem. My Mom took me to different doctors and I had a variety of tests done. As it turns out, I could hear perfectly fine and I could speak perfectly fine. I just chose not to speak. I always thought this was fascinating. I made up a variety of conclusions to my mute personality. At one point in my life I thought of myself as an observer and I was just taking everything in. At another point in my life, I thought that perhaps I wasn't fully on the planet yet. I thought maybe I was only partly here, but my soul was off doing work somewhere else in a different time. It took reading a book on adult ADHD in my second year of university that I really began to think about this experience being linked to something new.

First of all, I must be honest I never actually read the book. I tried to read the book. What happened was I would start reading and then I would feel hungry, so I would go and get something to eat. I would sit down again to read it and then the phone would ring. After my phone call I would clean up the dishes, have a shower, check my emails and watch some YouTube videos. I would sit down again to read the book and I would get through a couple of pages, but then it was time to go to work. So I would bring the book with me in case it was slow at work. At times it would get slow at work, I would read a paragraph or two and then go serve a table. I would make a couple of coffees and then read another paragraph. I would decide to clean the condiments and realize we were out of ketchup. So then I would go downstairs to get some more, but end up cleaning the boxes down there. Time flew by and my shift was over. I would clean up and close up. I would go home to read the book while I rested in bed and then I would fall asleep. I thought a day like this was normal for people. As it turns out, the more I would read in this book, the more it would trigger reflection within me. It was the first time I realized there was a serious chance that I had ADHD. I was twenty years old! How did I not know that?

I never finished the book. I wrote a whole paper on the fact that I could not get through the book and everything I did read it would trigger a new realization about myself that I had never considered before. I got an A+++ on this paper. Sincerely, I never finished the book and I still have yet to finish the book. I believe my bookmark still holds the spot where I stopped. My professor loved the paper and wrote a message on it to make an appointment if I needed to talk about what the book brought up for me. I followed up and made an appointment, but I still really didn't understand what this new realization was going to do for me. It was always just the way it was. I didn't know that people did not experience life in the way that I did. I would hate for any of my professors or university classmates to read this now, but I never did finish a book in university. Not one. I was also a top student. If I received a B on something, I was upset. I was extremely hard on myself and did extremely well. If I had to write a paper for marks, I did really well. I soaked up every word that professors would share in class, learned their opinions and just wrote about them. Or I would meet up with other students and discuss books and assignments and learn through our discussions. Writing papers was no problem, but if I had to write an exam, I did horrible. I was not the kid that could sit and read a book, memorize the information and then sit and read through multiple-choice questions and pick one. By the time I got to answer "E- All of the above", I could not even recall what the question was. Writing exams was extremely stressful for me. The rooms that we wrote exams in were usually massive, filled with people experiencing high anxiety, and although it was meant to be quiet, the room was loud. Any movement would easily distract me, even a person erasing an answer on their own paper. When someone would finish and hand in their exam, my anxiety would shoot through the roof because I wasn't even half way through. It was unreal how anxious I would get. I would start to sweat, my body would start to shake, and I would get dizzy and feel faint. I would read and re-read questions and answers over and over and over again. Finally, I would get to a point where I would just answer 'Cs'. One exam I wrote, I didn't even read the questions and answers anymore, I just guessed the letters and circled them. I got sixty percent on the exam. I was pretty impressed with myself for having just guessed!

What I learned from reading pieces of this book is that most people with ADHD have also experienced trauma in their infancy; the research demonstrates that the two are linked. When I first read that, I reflected on my childhood and thought to myself that I had a great childhood. I had loving parents who raised me and I could not recall any type of trauma that I could have experienced. After some thought, I realized that I was an infant when my uncle committed suicide. Many people may look to this experience and simply disregard that an infant could not possibly have been affected by a suicide at such an age. After working with children's mental health for the past five years, I have developed a better understanding of the impact an environment, as well as the relationships and attachments during this time of infancy can have on the development of a child's brain. My uncle was not only my Dad's brother and my mom's brother-in-law, but also, he was a dear friend to my mom and like an older brother/father figure to my five-year-old brother at the time. He was around all the time and had a special relationship to my closest family members. Losing a member of the family, a close friend and a role model, of course had an impact on my whole family. Those who surrounded me were in pain, grieving and mourning a dear loss. That alone can affect a child and the parent-child attachment relationship.

In addition to that realization, through a variety of meditations and healing treatments to explore my subconscious mind, I have developed a better understanding of how this experience had a real impact on me, even as an infant. My uncle came to our house before hand to talk to my mom. He had something he wanted to talk about but in that moment my mom was trying to take care of me and was preoccupied. He left, telling my mom he would talk about it afterwards. He committed suicide before my mom had a chance to talk to him again. I am sure my mom has worked out her own thoughts and feelings around this experience; however, as I mentioned, through self-exploration using meditation and understanding the subconscious mind, I have now realized that in my infancy, I decided that it was my fault that my uncle committed suicide. If my mom were not taking care of me, she would have been able to talk to him and maybe offered the support that he needed at the time. At this young age, I decided that the reason everyone was upset and grieving was because of me; therefore, it became my responsibility to make everyone else happy. It is quite a major decision to have made at such a young age. It may sound ludicrous and now looking back, I can see that it is. However, we all make decisions about the experiences we have and we make things that happen in these experiences mean something and more often than not, these decisions are held in our subconscious mind and dictate much of our conscious world.

I realize now that much of my world growing up was linked to this experience. I was always in search of what people needed to be happy. This quest served a purpose in my life and really allowed me to enjoy the journey of discovering what brings happiness to people. I have travelled most of the world and have developed a great understanding of people and various cultures. I have gone on amazing adventures and experienced amazing events. I wouldn't change a thing of my past. However, in understanding my subconscious mind, I know what the quest for happiness is linked to. I also understand that I made it mean that I cannot be happy unless everyone else is happy. Now that is ludicrous. This was a subconscious belief that put intense stress and worry on me that I could not understand. I would seek out all of the things that create happiness, taste that happiness, yet always be short of fully experiencing it, while never knowing why. I would be extremely excited and happy but go into periods of sadness and depression. I always worried about everyone else and everyone's wellbeing.

It is empowering to take time to develop an understanding of thoughts, beliefs, experiences, events, as well as the meanings and the decisions we make, even as young children; perhaps most importantly as young children. Self-reflection can create an opportunity to heal, to understand and to realize how everything within us and about us is linked. With this understanding we can make conscious decisions about which of these thoughts and beliefs are empowering for ourselves and which have been limiting or holding us back from being who we are truly meant to be.

I can now look back and be grateful for my quest for happiness and all the amazing experiences I have had through that. It may be linked to a belief I created when I was an infant; however, it served a purpose in my life for the time. Now I can reflect, let it go, and be grateful. I can look to the child within me and be assured that it wasn't my fault my uncle committed suicide and it is most definitely not my responsibility to make everyone else happy. It is my responsibility to focus on what makes me happy. As I learn how to enjoy and to live life with love, that can be shared with those around me, without the stress or worry about taking care of everyone else. People are on their own journey to seek their own happiness. As I learn and understand that, I can share with others how to learn and to understand their own journey as well. I can stop trying to subconsciously fix it for everybody! What a silly decision to have made at such a young age. No wonder why I didn't talk for the first three years of my life. I created a huge role for myself by taking on everyone else's burden! I clearly have enough luggage of my own to worry about. Can you see how sorting through that luggage is empowering and liberating?

Another piece of luggage I packed was much larger than the gym bag I kept under my window. It was for the first trip I took on my own without the family tribe. This first adventure was to Europe to teach English as a second language in Italy. I travelled with two friends from my University program. I wanted to make sure I had everything I needed. I asked the other two girls what they were bringing and what kind of luggage they had. They told me they were packing everything in one of the large, wheeled suitcases. Originally I wanted to pack everything in one smaller piece of luggage.   As it turns out, I wasn't just dealing with my own trip anxieties, I was dealing with my mother's as well. She assured me that I would need the large suitcase, which in our house is the size you would fit a sumo wrestler in if you were to pack one. To be honest, I don't even remember what I brought in that massive case. I likely brought my entire wardrobe, every pair of shoes I owned, and anything I thought I would ever need, ever. If I had luggage at four years old, you can only image the luggage I had when I was nineteen years old. In fact, I still packed a piece of my baby blanket, you know, a piece of home.

I will never forget that trip, because of my luggage. It was a valuable lesson. I was traveling around Italy– jumping on and off trains, hauling up cobbled pathways, squeezing through narrow halls, carrying my luggage up stairs of train stations, and lugging it down stairs on the other side. I was sweating, swearing, and frantically trying to bring this huge bag around with me everywhere I went. Not to mention, strangers were attempting to help me too, and they had difficulty! I promised myself that never again would I haul around this huge piece of luggage. After meeting people with a simple backpack on their back, I thought to myself, that will be the first thing I purchase before going anywhere ever again. It was excruciating hell.

It's always funny to think about things after the fact; you know, when you are no longer in the midst of the struggle or stupidity or silliness. Perhaps not so funny is the fact that we all have luggage that we are carrying around. We all have, what I like to call, our own invisible bag of bricks. Some of us haul them around, weighed down, exhausted and strained; while others walk along with a loaded bag propped up on their back. It doesn't matter the look or the size, we all have an invisible bag we lug around and some of us are completely unaware of it.

Our bag of bricks tends to be our experiences or our situations that weigh us down. Sometimes it's even our thoughts, beliefs or perspectives. It is like carrying the fear of the house burning down or fear of losing family members. It is carrying the decision that saving my family is my responsibility or that it was my mom's fault that I brought a huge piece of luggage to Italy. The truth is I had the choice myself. For me, it was also carrying the responsibility of making everyone close to me happy. It's all the "stuff" that gets in the way of us walking with ease, freely, carefree, fearlessly and joyfully, fully whole, as ourselves, comfortable in our own skin, content with who we are, where we have been, and what our life is all about. It's rare to find someone without some luggage to carry around.

It was when I left home for the first time to go experience the world that I realized that I had more "luggage" than I had actually packed. We have no idea that the way we were raised, the experiences we have or the culture that we grow up in, all create a range of outside factors that help to determine who we are.

Life goes a little bit like this. We are babies and our parents have the first opportunity to choose to influence us or not. Some parents decide it is best that someone else take over, maybe another family member or a foster family or an adoption agency. Some other parents take the challenge. Nonetheless, as children, we really rely on someone else to take care of things for us and to show us the way. Some of us are taught about God or Buddha or Allah. Some of us are taught to say please and thank you. Some of us are taught what anger and hate looks like. Some of us are taught what love and care looks like. All of us learn about the world around us at the time, which includes learning about the relationships of people that make up that world. When we are children everything taught to us becomes our truth. As we get older and grow up, we are exposed to some new influences. We start to become a little more open to other ideas and other truths. Some of these ideas and truths conflict with what we have already learned. Suddenly we are in a place left only to think, well what the fuck is true?

Once we become aware that everything we have ever known to be true could possibly mean something else, it can become frustrating or confusing. Beliefs that have dictated your life begin to come crashing down. Thoughts and ideas about things don't appear real anymore. Discovering what makes people happy drove my entire life for a good chunk of time. It gave me a sense of purpose and desire. Suddenly I recognized that it didn't matter what made people happy. Everyone is on their own journey and my attachment to their happiness is out of my control. If I live my life trying to make everyone else happy, essentially I will be unhappy. I have no control over anyone else except for myself. Letting go of a belief that has always been part of me was really difficult to do. It made up who I was. It was the essence of my relationships. It was the core of everything that I dd. I developed nuero pathways in my brain that supported that belief. My initial response was to go back to that belief system that made up so much of who I was, but I was committed to grow through it. It takes time to re-evaluate your thoughts and beliefs. It takes time to determine if they are working for you or if they are holding you back. It takes time to recondition new beliefs that are more empowering. Just because I let go of the subconscious belief that it is my responsibility to make people happy, that doesn't mean I'm never going to make people happy again! It just means I get to let go of the worry and attachment to an outcome that I really have no control over.

Many people think I travel to go find myself somewhere out there. I am where I am. For me, traveling was a gift that I gave myself, not to find myself, but to uncover who I really am. We are constantly bombarded with programming to feel that we need a certain product to be pretty, certain clothing to be skinny, certain food to be strong or certain medication to be sane. We are constantly being programmed to feel that we are not enough. We begin to believe it. Then we begin to tell ourselves the same message as well. We solidify that we are not enough. This results with looking outside of ourselves to find who we are. Eventually we feel unsatisfied because we have been there the whole time, unrecognized and dishonored. In addition, we have experiences that become defining moments in our decisions about the world around us, and what we decide about ourselves in that world. Some of these decisions can be empowering and some of these decisions can be limiting. I can't. I'm not good enough. I don't have money for that. It's my fault. I am this way because this event happened. It's my responsibility.

I don't have enough time. I'm not pretty, smart or rich enough. I'm not loved. I need to do this or not do that in order to be loved.

These are our bricks. We carry them around, unknowingly. We wander aimlessly through life in hopes someone will tell us which direction to go, what to do, when to eat, where to sit, when to finish, how to do it and when to stop. We are told how to feel happy, to feel good, to look good or to be better. It is constant. What's dangerous is we begin to believe it. Then we begin to rely on it to make us who we are. In doing this, we completely neglect that we are exactly who we are meant to be and we have exactly what we need already. We build ourselves with brick after brick. We carry our experiences like they are a burden; our emotions because we don't know how to express them; and our beliefs that were decided in moments when we didn't know better. This allows our bricks to make up who we are. Sadly, most of this is completely on a subconscious level. (So wake up!)

When I started exploring my invisible luggage, developing a better understanding of myself and venturing into my subconscious mind, examining my childhood and grasping a deeper understanding of who I am and how I came to get there, I discovered the reality of myself and made sense of it all. I can look at my past, from infancy, childhood, adolescence and early adulthood and really appreciate all my experiences- those experiences, which were challenging and painful to those experiences, which were enjoyable and miraculous. All of these events and relationships have helped shape my life and brought me to where I am today. I can be grateful for even the most difficult situations, because even those are gifts in life that shape who we are, the decisions we make and the path we choose to take. If life were always a joyous skip along the way, our stories wouldn't be interesting and growing through our challenges wouldn't be so fulfilling. Growing through our challenges allows us to learn and to grow stronger. Every story has conflict to make it more interesting. You write your own story. However, when conflict arises, you become the hero that chooses to overcome the challenge. Once we have a full understanding of how we came to be the person we are, we can become conscious of who we are and conscious of who we would like to be.

We don't always have to carry around that invisible luggage once we have an understanding of it. We can understand what bricks we are carrying. We can choose to continue carrying that weight around, or choose lay the bricks down. As we grow through our story, we can choose what works for us, what empowers us and what tools can be used from our experiences. We do not have to carry our world on our backs. Our luggage can change and it doesn't have to become heavier and heavier as we continue on. We choose what bricks we want to carry or if we choose to carry bricks at all. We are meant to stand on the world, not carry it. We must place each brick, experience, emotion, belief, and challenge down into the foundation at our feet so we can stand tall on top of it all. This allows us to overcome what we thought were struggles by becoming the master of our life through understanding who we are and who we are meant to be. We all experience challenges in our lives. We can choose to suffer from those experiences, by carrying our luggage and having it hold us down or we can choose to grow from those experiences, using our bricks to stand upon, walking forward with ease, with empowerment and with joy.

Anyone who grows a garden tends to lay down a layer of manure into the soil, which helps a plant to grow stronger, by providing nutrients, minerals and organic matter. Our bag of bricks is like carrying around our own bag of manure. Sometimes it really stinks; however, we can learn to use our manure to fertilize who we are meant to be. When we grow through our manure we only grow stronger and flourish. Life can appear to be a real stinky drag if we choose not to explore what's in our luggage. We can choose to keep carrying it around or we can choose to lay down our manure, nourishing ourselves into who we are meant to be. Once we grow into who we are meant to be, we grow our buds or fruits in order to share with others. We root into the earth, grow tall, stand strong and be all we are meant to be, then we contribute back and share with those around us.

e Exercise

ect on defining experiences you had from childhood till now. Close your eyes an.. *ualize yourself in each experience. How did you feel in that moment? How did you feel just before that experience? What did you decide in the moment of that experience? How has this had an impact on who you are today?*

Take a moment and think about all the bricks weighing you down. What experiences, situations, or emotions do you feel you have been carrying around? What types of limiting beliefs have been programmed within you that you were or were not aware of? Unload your bricks by writing them onto a piece paper. Have a look at them. Think about where they might have come from. Is this the first time you have noticed these bricks?

Revealing your own bricks is an ongoing practice. It is not just a one-time deal. Allow yourself to reveal other bricks as you continue your journey through this book and add to your list. Become aware of your bricks and your limiting beliefs. Some days we tend to carry a larger piece of luggage than other days, but just for today, leave your luggage behind you.

If you feel a bit lighter, leave it again tomorrow.

THE PASSPORT

Passport photos always crack me up. I have yet to see a passport photo that really reflects who a person is. Most photos look like a criminal mug shot, rarely ever looking like the person who owns the passport. I do not understand why we cannot just smile for the photo. After all, we are typically getting a passport in order to go somewhere for a holiday; that must be worth a smile!

It appears to me that the passport itself can reflect a person more so than the photo alone. A new passport is like a blank canvas. It is empty and waiting for its soul to be created. We have many choices to make with a new passport. Where can I go? What can I see? How can this canvas be created? Some people fill their passport in the time period before it expires, others create a page or two, and some people do not even own a passport. A full passport can tell stories of inspiration, challenges, excitement and thrill.

We have a choice you know, whether to get a passport or not and of course, whether to fill the passport or not. Some people are stuck in a limiting belief like, "I don't have enough money." This, like many others, is a limiting belief because it assumes that an outside source dictates our life. If you do not have money to travel, then find a way to receive or make money. It fascinates me to encounter people who work and then spend all their money on clothing and shoes or drinks and food out on the weekends. They look great, sit around a table and share with me that they wish they traveled somewhere. Traveling is not for the elite only. Traveling is available to anyone. It's not about having the right resources or enough finances. It is about being resourceful and determining a way to simply just make it happen. It is our limiting beliefs that get in the way of us doing things we desire or wish to do. Not having enough money is just one limiting belief that is given power to hold us back.

Our limiting beliefs of the world or things we have determined as our 'truths' get in the way of our choices. We are bombarded with many outside influences that help to determine who we are; however, we can choose to be one of those influences. We can choose what influences us. We can choose if our photos are going to look like a prisoner in a jail cell or if it's going to look like a person going on a holiday.

Often we look to things that we have no control over to fog our ability to choose our own life. Even when everything feels like it is totally and utterly out of our control or it appears that everyone else has control over our life and we cannot do anything about it, get this, we still have control. In fact, in life, no matter what we encounter we have control over three things: what we think, what we say, and what we do. We are constantly making choices in these three areas. First we choose what we think about or what we focus on. Secondly, we choose the words we speak and how we choose to speak them. Lastly, we choose how we can respond in our life or react.

Our choices determine who we are and what we do. Every moment we are making a decision. Our thoughts are a significant part of our decision making. What we are focusing on is the most important thing in the world to us, because we are present and focusing on it. When we focus on problems, negative experiences and lower energy emotions, we tend to generate more negative themes in our lives. That is all we are focusing on. Seek and you shall find. If you seek all the things that are going wrong in life you will find more of them to complain about. If you seek all of the things to be grateful for or that make you happy then, hey, you will notice more of that positive theme growing in your life. Noticing more good generates more good in our lives. Energy following thought is not just wishful thinking; it is a law of the universe. Our focus creates what we think about. Our thoughts create our emotions. Our emotions generate energy within the law of attraction. For example, if our focus is on love, we will create the emotion of love. This emotion will be radiated through the energy of our body and generate more love. If our focus is on fear, we will create the emotion of fear. This emotion will radiate through the energy of our body and generate more fear. You can choose where to focus; you can choose love or fear. It can be simplified by these two options because everything else is a branch of either love or a branch of fear. You choose love or fear based on where you choose to focus your thoughts on.

It is important to be aware of the thoughts you are creating about the world around you, as well as the thoughts you are creating about yourself. Are you constantly beating yourself up in you head, going over all of the things you should have done, could have done, or didn't do? Are you putting yourself down, insulting yourself, or telling yourself how stupid, fat or ugly you are? Or is the conversation you have with yourself coming from a place of understanding, compassion and gentleness? Do you indulge yourself with self-love? Do you encourage yourself, compliment yourself and remind yourself how amazing, beautiful and talented you are? Be mindful of how you think about yourself and the world around you. The way you think about things will reflect the way you see things and likely reflect the joy or lack of joy in your life.

We are constantly bombarded with advertisements that shape how we think about the world or about ourselves. For the most part, advertisements make us feel as though there is something missing in our lives or keeping us from being "perfect" or "happy". This is strategic, of course, because the advertisement replaces that feeling of not being enough, with having the product they sell in order to be whole, beautiful, perfect and strong. What if we became our own advertisement? What if we became an influence in how we think and feel? What would that look like? It could start with the mere thought that everything we need we already have. We know everything we need to know and we know exactly what to do to learn more with ease, joy and gratitude. Everything we dream the world to be can exist and the steps to making dreams a reality start right here in this moment. It begins with the thought.

What if we changed our focus to be on the things we can control in our lives in order to make our lives happier and more fulfilling? It is just a switch. Becoming mindful of our thoughts, where we focus and how we use that focus to empower ourselves rather than to limit ourselves is the first step. We can come from one of two places, a place of love or a place of fear. We are making decisions every moment that shape who we are and how we live our life. What have you been focusing on?

Our decisions shape our life. Deciding to wake up in the morning, to shower and to get dressed will help to determine if we leave the house and go to school or work or meet up with someone we know. Showing up to an event or gathering will determine if we have a certain conversation that will provide us with information or offer a conversation of care and love. Choosing to turn right instead of going straight can determine if we miss an accident. Choosing a shirt that attracts the attention of someone who asks for a date can determine the beginning of a lasting relationship. Choosing to get behind a wheel after drinking and getting into an accident can dictate the life of someone ending or continuing. Choosing to stop and to help someone can demonstrate an act of love that stops that person from pulling a trigger to his or her temple. Choosing to be mindful of eating healthy food can determine the energy you have for the day and the information you soak up and learn. Choosing to show up for your life can provide you an opportunity to create a magnificent story. Choosing to focus on love can dictate the joy and happiness you experience through the day and for your life. Every moment you are making a decision that dictates your life and has the potential to make a seriously important impact on another person's life as well.

Our words also reflect who we are and what we are focusing on. We can think positively for hours, pump ourselves up and be our own advertisement in our mind and in one five minute conversation with someone, complain about a situation we are part of, or insult someone we know or say out loud, 'oh I'm so stupid, I don't know why I did that.'

What terrifies me is how people speak to those they love. People insult the people they love, swear at them jokingly, put them down or become an advertisement in their life that feeds the belief that they are not good enough. Do we really need to wonder where bullies come from when so many people speak to the people they love in this way? Why would anyone have compassion, understanding and gentleness with people they don't like if they barely have it for people that they love? Sadly, this is all linked to the fact that people do not have compassion, understanding and gentleness for themselves. If someone does not experience self-love, how can anyone really experience love for another?

We have many people in our lives that model love in different ways. Sometimes we see that love comes out in violence, abuse or pressure. I hit you because I love you. I pressure you to do something you don't want to do because it will show that you love me. If you don't, you clearly don't love me. What is even more terrifying to me is the fact that we really believe these messages. The reason we believe these messages is typically because at a young age we made a decision about the world around us, perhaps we decided that we are not worthy or not loveable. We can look at the world around us with spite, anger or defeat. Or instead, like a switch, we can change the way we look to the world around us, with love, compassion and understanding. Others may express love in many ways. We may not have a role model in our life that reflects self-love or love for others; however, we can choose to become that role model. You can be your own role model of what love looks like.

Energy follows thought and energy is within our words. Our words carry the sound frequency that determines our perspective of the world around us. We must be mindful of the sounds that we create. Being aware of the words we choose to describe ourselves, our lives and the world around us will help to shape who we are and how we see in the world. The songs we listen to and the songs we sing carry a frequency that generates thought and emotion within us. Are we listening and singing songs that generate anger, sadness and pain? Are we listening and singing songs that generate love, joy and excitement? These are part of the words we are choosing to speak and to sing. These sound frequencies connect to the energy within and around us and this helps to shape the world around us.

We can choose in our mind to be happy and we can use our words to affirm our happiness, but we must also master our actions. Learning how to respond to situations that arise, instead of reacting is a significant tool that we have control of. Is it helpful to blow up with anger or to shut down and isolate? Is it helpful to turn to an outside source to meet our needs, such as cigarettes, food, alcohol or drugs? In our mind we have decided that these things help, but in addition, we have trained our body to respond to use these coping strategies. It has become part of our nervous system. We have programmed our own bodies to respond in the way that matches the beliefs that were an influence on us. This is important to understand as well, because it becomes more than just being mindful of your thoughts and your words; we must become mindful of our physical body and how it has learned to support our thoughts and words, which can be both empowering or disempowering. Our thoughts and words help to create our emotions and our body responds to the learned behavior of supporting these emotions. When I am sad I turn to alcohol. When I am angry I must physically break something. When I am discouraged I isolate myself. When I am depressed I sleep. When I am bored I eat. When I do not like what I am doing I create a problem. When I am stressed I smoke. When I am tired I drink coffee. We have so many emotions we react with that have created neuropaths in our brain to respond in a certain way. Many of us are unaware of these ways we have conditioned our-selves to respond with. Many of us can name what we do when we feel a certain way; however, we are limited in thinking that it ends there. We have control over how we respond, based on understanding that we can control our thoughts and focus, ultimately controlling our emotions. We do not need to continue conditioning these unhelpful patterns. We can interrupted those patterns and condition new, empowering patterns. Once this understanding is developed, it is a matter of deciding how you will choose to control your thought focus in order to control your emotions.

As we are growing up, no matter the age, we have the potential to be growing. In fact, if we are not growing, we are dying. We experience a whole range of emotions as human beings. Unfortunately, no one ever explains to us that emotions are normal or how to understand our emotions. Instead we are told we can only be happy. When we don't feel happy we feel like something is wrong with who we are. Yet, emotions are part of who we are and, get this, emotions are okay! However, emotions do not define who we are. Emotions indicate that we feel something. We can choose to feel our emotions and we do not have to be scared to feel. It is okay to be sad, angry, frustrated or mad. It is okay! It is important to be aware of how we choose to understand and to show that emotion. We can be angry and choose to yell, swear, throw things and renovate the house with holes in the wall. Or we can notice the feeling of anger, sit with it and understand it. We can be sad, depressed and shut off from the world, in isolation, becoming even more down. Or we can allow ourselves the time and space to cry and let it out, and again, understand the sadness. Once we understand our emotions, on our own, we can choose to communicate to others in a more respect-ful and clear way, instead of unleashing our first reaction.

Sometimes we feel emotions and we have no idea why. We need to stop and figure out the why. What's going on here? Where is this coming from? What is this linked to? When we seek with curiosity, we can develop a better understanding. This is a gift we give to ourselves and it is a gift we give to the world. Our emotions can be used to empower ourselves or to limit ourselves. When we can master our emotions, we can use them to support who we really are. Anger, frustra-tion and even fear can be the driving force to create change for the good. Sadness, depression, and hurt can create compassion, understanding and insight. Insight can create the steppingstones out of these lower energies and into a place of empowerment. When we understand our own emotions, we can begin to understand other people and how their emotions are also driving forces. For example, we can review the situation of a bully. The anger and fear in the bully, has created the bully's way of thinking and the bully's way of being. A bully has learned that he/she must make someone else feel insignificant in order to feel significant. The bully doesn't need punishment; instead the bully needs love and understanding. The so-called "victim" being bullied, is not a victim, because no one is a victim. This is just a person who already believes that he/she is insignificant and someone else who comes around to enhance that insignificance just enforces that belief. And the bystanders? Well, they are just relieved that they are not the ones being told they are insignificant, because they likely already believe that too.

The truth is, bullying doesn't just happen in the playground. Bullying is a major part of our society as a whole. People are made up of limiting beliefs that make them feel insignificant and they go outside themselves to feel significant. However, it's like a switch, we can choose how to make ourselves feel significant right now, in this moment, with the decisions we make; choosing how we think, what we focus on, the words we speak and how we choose to respond to the world around us. It begins in this moment, with each of us, as individuals. How you think about yourself will become who you are. Be kind, be gentle, and love yourself as you are. Understand who that is and determine ways to change to make yourself be the person you would want to look up to. When you can choose to think, to speak and to respond to yourself with love, care, compassion, gentleness and understanding, you will learn how to respond to the people and the world around you in this same way. Imagine that, in a world that can be a struggle, unfair, unjust or for some unbearable, we can still choose to think, speak and act from a place of love, kindness, gentleness, compassion, and understanding. It is possible.

We must understand our emotions because they reveal where we are as individuals. If we are constantly upset, angry and frustrated, this is an indicator of where our thoughts and words are focused. If we are feeling happy, loving, joyous and blissful, this is an indicator of where our thoughts and words are focused. We think emotions create who we are; however, we create our emotions. This is an extremely important concept to explore. Where we place our thoughts, our focus, and our words determines our emotions. Our thought and sound frequencies generate how we physically feel and help to determine the actions we choose to respond with or decisions we make to shape our life.

Sometimes emotions surface that need to be explored and understood in order to grow and to heal. That's okay too. Sitting with an emotion to understand it can be helpful. A situation may occur that makes you angry. We may think it is the situation that caused the anger; however, most times the situation created an opportunity to surface anger within that needs exploration and understanding. You determine how long you want to sit with an emotion based on what you focus on.

In short, we can choose to focus on one of two options: love or fear. When we choose to focus on thoughts, words and actions of love, we will generate the emotion of love within ourselves, while generating that emotion for others to feel. When we choose to focus on thoughts, words and actions of fear, we will generate the emotions linked to fear within ourselves, which generates that emotion for others to feel. In the past, generation after generation, for thousands of years, humans have generated a world of fear. I encourage you to wake the love up within you and watch as we wake the love up in the world around us. Love is like a lit candle in a dark room. Even when the room is filled with darkness, the entire focus goes to that lit candle. That candle can shine bright enough for us to find another candle to light. As a few more candles are lit within that dark room, the light switch can be found and the room can be lit entirely. Fear, or darkness cannot enter a lit room to have any impact whatsoever. I don't know about you, but I'd like to take part in lighting up our world.

When you choose to focus on thoughts, words and actions of love, you choose to be that lit candle. Soon you begin to light other candles and eventually the whole room can be lit up. Sometimes your candle will burn out, but by that time, other candles surround you and help to light you up again. Eventually the light switch is found and you are surrounded and filled with light. You no longer need to rely on your wick; you just become the light and it just becomes the world around you. This is love. This is the world you can create around you and the world we can collectively create to live in. This is directly related to the decisions we make moment to moment, day to day. Choose to focus on love and begin with self-love. Generate that love within you and fear can no longer dwell in your home. Your mind, body and heart are your home. You choose how to decorate it. After all is said and done, it falls into one choice: love or fear.

Imagine, as you choose to fill your passport, radiating love, joy, compassion, understanding, gentleness, and joy wherever you go, every country, every stop, every friend you make, you share this gift. It's a secret. It is called world peace and it begins with you. You can create peace by enjoying the process of filling your passport. Happiness is not having a full passport to show you have gone and seen all these remarkable places. Happiness is found in the whole process. It begins by choosing to get a passport, smiling for the photo, and then receiving the passport in the mail. It continues by choosing a place to visit, packing, getting the passport stamped, and arriving to your set destination. Happiness is about experiencing the trip that generates the memories each time you look at that stamp once you have returned home. Happiness is the entire process of the journey, understanding each experience as a gift given along the way. Sharing those gifts collected along the way with others will only magnify the experience of happiness. Happiness, joy, bliss or peace is never the end result; but how you choose to think, to speak and to be during the whole process can be the ongoing result. Will your passport be filled with love or will fear stop you from even getting a passport?

Eagle Exercise:

Begin to notice what kinds of conversations you have in your head. How do you think about yourself or about the world around you? Do your thoughts come from a place of love? Begin to notice the words you use. How do you speak with or to others? Do you criticize or do you encourage? Do you engage in fear-based conversation?

What emotions are you experiencing most frequently on a day-to-day basis? How does this reflect what you are focusing on? How does this affect your thoughts and your words?

Just for today, monitor your thoughts, words and actions. Focus on thinking and speaking words of love. If you go back to the negative again, just notice and replace it with something loving. If you notice a difference in your thinking, try again tomorrow.

THE DEPARTURE

I truly feel there is a distinct line between people who want to travel and people who want to travel but don't. The distinct line is the departure. I feel there is always a reason not to go. Some people think it is money or time, others think it is their job, family or current situation. There are many reasons not to travel, however, the people who do travel tend to seek out the reasons to go and to take that leap.

Most times we are thrilled to get out of where we are and to jump into the excitement of visiting a new place and experiencing a different way of life. Yet, right at the point of departure, everything you really like about where you are will tend to be magnified. It's as though it is a test to determine how much you really want to experience that something new. The going is not the difficult part, the leaving is.

For me, my nephew is the most difficult part of leaving. I simply adore him. I miss him when I don't see him for a couple of days, let alone for a long period of time while I am traveling. We have such a special connection. I always feel close to him, however, when I travel, we can't run, play and soak up every second together. It's different and I don't like it. Leaving my nephew is always the most difficult thing for me to do.

In addition, every single trip I ever embark upon involves my Mom ignoring the fact that I am going anywhere, right up until the day I start packing. In the week of my departure she gets this look on her face as though it has suddenly occurred to her that I am leaving somewhere. The look of pure sadness in her eyes shows she's going to have an extra load of worry until the day I arrive home again. We can barely talk about the trip because there is too much uncertainty for her to know that I am going to be fine, so she gives it up to God. She hounds the angels, the saints and anyone else she can possibly think of in the spirit world to protect me and to keep me safe. She prays and prays and prays in order to replace the gut wrenching feeling of worry with faith.

My Dad deals with it a little differently. He tends to crack jokes like I can't be leaving soon enough. I know he's really saying, "I'll miss you", especially when he helps me find the right utility knife to bring for the adventure or helps me to find something I am looking for. He calls me crazy, but he always hugs me a little longer than usual just before I go.

My brother's excitement always encourages me and reminds me of the reasons why I am going. I know if he felt like he could come, he'd be right next to me on every adventure. Most times I feel like he is. My family and friends all respond differently, some making it harder to go than others. The first couple of trips held an unspoken tension, like a cloud in a blue sky. People worry and people care. Now, with most of my friends it is as though they are conditioned to accept that I am going on a trip. The worry is still there for some, but now it's just what Laura does.

Departing for a trip is facing my greatest fear. It is not the act of going somewhere; it is the act of leaving something behind– specifically someone behind. My greatest fear is to lose someone close to me. What if something happens to someone I love so much and I am not here for it? It is a fear that sits in the back of my head and it's the heaviness in the bottom of my stomach. Fear of facing the greatest pain I think there is, losing someone you love. The pain is great. I have experienced what it means to lose someone close and I know I could not do anything about it. And the truth is, we cannot do anything about losing someone close to us, whether we are here or not. We may get caught up in pain and grief and convince ourselves that maybe if we said what we needed to say or if we were there they would not have gone that way or chosen this way. We can definitely get caught up in a cloud of sadness and feel as though we could have done something differently. Maybe you truly believe that you could have done something to change the way it worked out, and maybe you could have. If that is what you believe and you didn't do what you think you could have done, than you are not just left with fear, you are left with regret. Both will hold you back or give you the power to push through.

Fear and regret. Sometimes fear is what stops us from doing something we would really love to do. Afterwards we are left only to regret that we never did it. How do we avoid such pain? Perhaps it's not about avoiding the pain, but about using it as a force of empowerment.

Everyone has hopes, dreams and desires that inspire them. What separates people from actually living out their hopes, dreams and desires is the mere step in overcoming fear. This means pushing through into the life they desire to live. My fear of losing someone close, against the regret I may feel if I didn't follow through with my heart's passion, was something I needed to overcome in order to live my life to its fullest potential. I was successful, but along the way I experienced a major setback that required me to live out my greatest fear.

The fear of losing someone close has always been subtly evident in my life. I hated change since I was a child. When my parents went out, I used to sit at the window, praying that they were safe, anxiously wondering when they were going to return. My anxiety was extremely high for a young child and anxiety became part of me in my years of growing up. It didn't define me, but it was always there. I always had walls up in my intimate relationships. I thought it was the fear of getting hurt, but really it was the fear of losing someone I loved. This fear also plays a role in shaping the person who I am. I feel very strongly about saying what I think or feel in the moment because we really never know when we'll have another chance to do so. I don't like it when things are not peaceful. I prefer to solve conflict immediately rather than sit with a grudge or be angry. I grew up with the belief that life is short, so I attempted to live out every moment to its fullest. I learned to tell people I love them when I feel it and I learned to tell people I appreciated them when I am grateful. Think these traits were just part of who I am? Perhaps these traits were just in my genetic makeup, or perhaps this was also linked to the fact that I lost a close family member in my infancy. Experiences in our lives, no matter at what age, can have a major impact on how we choose to see the world. What we choose to make those experiences mean can subconsciously determine a lifetime of decisions.

One of my greatest dreams was to live in New York City for a period of time. I am Canadian so I had to find a legitimate way to make it happen. I applied to an Au Pair program to nanny for a family in New York. After exploring some options of families in New York, a family from Los Angeles requested that I consider L.A. instead of New York. The mother of three-year-old twins was a judge and did an excellent job convincing me that L.A. had many things that New York had, but the sun shone warmly and more often than in the Big Apple. After much discussion back and forth, I agreed to match up with the family in L.A. I looked forward to some big city fun in the sun.

I travelled to Haiti for the first time the week before I was scheduled to move to L.A. for a year. The trip itself completely took my perspective on life and expanded it beyond what I would have ever imagined. In short, the experience made an incredible impact on me. I decided that I needed to focus on making a change in the world that didn't allow for people to live in poverty. How is that okay? I was immediately grounded, humbled and grateful for absolutely every detail in my life. I could write a book on Haiti and international development on its own. I asked myself how I was going to go from visiting Haiti to moving to Los Angeles. Talk about rags to riches. While I was away, I decided that it didn't matter where I was, I could reach out to people in need. I decided I would find a place to volunteer or to help out while I lived in LA. I loved visiting the children at the orphanages in the hospitals. Perhaps I could do some clown doctor work in the children's ward at a hospital in LA. It didn't matter what I did, I just knew I needed to do something.

The Departure

When I arrived home from Haiti, I literally had to unpack my bag and re-pack it to leave in the same night. I was heading back to the airport to depart to New York for the Au Pair training that weekend. I would be in LA to meet my new family for the year that following Monday. Everything was pretty chaotic and I only had so much time to get home, switch everything over and head back to the airport. My mom had been acting weird, but as I mentioned, that is normal for her when I am off somewhere. It wasn't until we were off that she told me that my best friend's mom had died. My friend's mom had been pushing through the battle of cancer and although 'anytime' was, well, anytime, I was still shocked to hear the news. I was completely dumbfounded. I told my mom I had to stay, yet I had no one to contact at the Au Pair agency because it was in the middle of the night. When I think about it now, I don't know why it mattered, but it was so important for me that the Au Pair people needed to know that I couldn't be there and had to be home. Yet, I went through the motions. I sat in an airport, surrounded by business people in suits. Their suits were all black, as if they knew the women who had become like a second mom to me had died. I felt like I needed to cry, but I didn't have any emotions, I just moved through motions. I got on the plane and arrived at another airport. Some guy with a sign picked me up. I arrived to the hotel and was greeted by one of the Au Pair training facilitators. She introduced herself and I told her I needed to go home because my aunt died.

It just came out of my mouth. I don't know why I said aunt. What difference would it make if it were an aunt or a second mom? It's pretty much the same thing anyway. The lady, and I couldn't tell you her name, was so supportive. She told me we could contact my family in LA and look up the flights to head back home. I had to sit and wait. I don't know what I was waiting for, but I remember sitting and listening to someone talk about the American culture. She was talking about how no one ever says goodbye at the end of a conversation. She was explaining that some cultures say one quick bye and the conversation is over. However, in America, a person will say I have to go, and then start planning the next time to talk. Or instead of bye, a person might say see you later, even if that doesn't mean see you later. A person might say talk to you soon, even though they don't know when soon is. I don't know why this person had to talk about saying goodbye for so long, but it felt like I was sitting there for hours, listening about the American culture never saying goodbye.

I wished we never had to say goodbye. I remembered the last time I talked to my friend's mom. She told me to take care of her daughter. I told her I would, but I was in New York and she was somewhere else in misery. I knew I had to do whatever I needed to do to get back there. Yet I wondered what I would possibly do that was going to make a difference when I arrived. I didn't know how to make cookies like her mom. I wish I knew how to make those cookies. I miss them. She always gave me cookies when I was over there. She was a health nut, but cookies and chocolate were never low in stock at their house.

The Au Pair facilitator, I really I wish I remembered her name, was like an earth angel guiding me through the motions. I thought I was being tough and strong, but I think I was just in shock or maybe I was in denial. I thought maybe when I got home, it would all just be a lie and I would get to their house and instead we'd just eat cookies and laugh about how I wasn't in New York. Maybe I would wake up and it would all just be a dream. Then we'd analyze it and talk about what we thought it really meant. But it wasn't a dream. It was a nightmare and I wasn't waking up. The Earth Angel told me we needed to let my LA family know that I wouldn't be getting there when I was scheduled to. I told her that I didn't think the mom would be happy about the whole thing, but the Earth Angel assured me it would be fine and they would sort it out.

The judge was not happy at all. She wanted to know when I was going to be back. She told me it was a complete inconvenience on so many people that I wasn't arriving on time. She wanted to know who was going to pick up her kids after school on Monday. She ranted about how she had all kinds of meetings to cancel because of this. I thought I was tough and strong, but I think I was just in shock. It's like her words meant nothing to me. I just got back from Haiti where children die because they do not receive human touch; it's a place where the average person only makes one dollar a day. I had just spent over a week feeling guilty to eat because so many were starving. Yet, she wanted to know who was going to pick up her kids? Somehow I had compassion. I just told her I was sorry that this experience was such an inconvenience. I think that's what I said. I know I didn't say much, I don't really remember. I just listened. The Earth Angel just stared at me with tears in her eyes. After the conversation she told me that if I wanted to match up with a new family that she would back up my decision. I told her it was no problem and we'd sort it out. I went to my room. I sat there for five minutes and went back to see the Earth Angel. I told her that I didn't want to be paired up with that family anymore. I understood the mom was upset, but I thought to myself if she didn't have understanding for a death, I don't know what else she could have an understanding for. And that was that. I never heard from the family again. Instead, I booked a flight out of New York to return home first thing in the morning.

I called my friend that night. She was mad. She was really mad. She couldn't understand how her best friend was in New York when her mom had just died. It was as though all of her emotion of losing her mother was wrapped in the fact that her best friend wasn't there. She just threw it all at me. I thought I was tough and strong, but I think I was just in shock. I didn't say much to her either, I just listened. I'm glad I don't remember that conversation either. I just knew I needed to go home, so I did. Once I got there, I showed up at her house, not knowing how mad she was going to be, but instead she asked how I got there and we just hugged. Sometimes there are no words.

I have attended too many funerals for my age. The first was my Great Grandmother when I was just a kid. I walked in and saw her in the coffin and that was it for me. Why didn't anyone warn me about that? It's the first thing you see, when you walk in and as a kid, you are eye-to-eye with the person in bed. This time I was 22 years old and I attended too, too many funerals that year. My friend's mom was number three in March. Once a month for the first nine months of that year, I was at the funeral home. I knew the people who worked there by name and wondered if I should just apply for a job.

After the motions of my friend's mom's funeral, I found myself at home. I had nothing to do. I quit my jobs before I left. I completed all the things I thought needed to be done before I took off for the year.

I ended up getting my job back at a Community Girls' Home. I returned in a week and joked that I had just 'fake quit'. That was only part time work. I spent quite a bit of time in my head– a little too much time in my head. I started to get down and depressed. I wondered what my purpose was and what I was suppose to do with my life. The Au Pair company said they would contact me in a few weeks to set me up with a new family. I began to wonder if I even wanted a new family. I already had a family. Couldn't I just get a private jet and fly back and forth to New York through the week? I thought about Haiti quite a bit as well. I felt down and depressed, but I didn't know why. I felt pretty damn grateful too. Oddly enough, Haiti can do that to you. I was really grateful for everything in my life and for everyone. I decided that I was going to write letters to people I was grateful to for being part of my life. I wanted people in my life who have always been there for me, to know that I was thankful for them. I got some cards and started writing notes to those people and mailed them. I wanted to let those people know that I acknowledged their care, that I appreciated them and that I loved them. The week I mailed those cards out was the week my Aunt completed suicide.

I had just arrived at my Grandparents' house when my Nonna was on the phone screaming, "She's dead!" in Italian. I looked at her and asked who she was talking about. She told me my Grandfather was at my Aunt Sara's house and he found her dead. I was out the door and on the phone with 911, racing in my car, trying to remember the address of her house so I could tell the dispatcher. I was calm and answering the women's questions, but I didn't appear to have any answers. I couldn't remember the street name, let alone the house number. I couldn't tell her what happened I just knew she was dead. Or maybe she wasn't dead? I got to the house and called 911 from her landline so they would get the house information. We were left to wait. I asked him where she was and if he was sure she was dead. He said she was upstairs and asked if I wanted to double check. I went upstairs and she was in her bed. I checked her pulse. She was cold and she was dead. I knelt down beside her and said a prayer then went downstairs to wait for the emergency response team. It felt like hours. That's when I found her notes, scrib-bled on notepad, on the table and on the floor, where pills were also scattered, dropped and untouched on the kitchen floor. I started to gather the notes off the floor and the table and that's when I saw my card that I had wrote to her. It was in the pile of her mail. The card was unopened.

I just looked at it. It stared back at me. You would think that seeing a dead body, a suicide note and pills in every direction would have had more of an impact, but no, apparently not for me. Seeing the card unopened was like a knife slicing across my throat. In that card I told her how much she meant to me. I told her how grateful I was to have her in my life. I told her that she was always my number one fan. She always saw my bright light and always thought I was someone special. But in that card I told her she was someone special to me. Next to my mom, she is the only other person that showed up for absolutely everything I ever did. And next to my mom she always was. She was her aunt too. She was her aunt, her best friend, her sister-figure, her mother-figure, her greatest button pusher, her greatest teacher, her partner in crime, her guru, her... everything. She was my Great Aunt Sara and great she was. She was more than great and that's why I wrote the card in the first place.

Maybe if she opened the card and knew how much she meant to me, than maybe she wouldn't have killed herself. Maybe if she knew how much she meant to all of us and how destroyed we would be to lose her, than maybe she wouldn't have killed herself. Why did she get the mail, but not open the card? Why did she just leave it there, on the table, beside the note she wrote? She must have sat right beside it, why didn't she just read it? Maybe if she read the card, maybe she wouldn't have killed herself. Why didn't I send the cards earlier? Why did I procrastinate? Why didn't I just call her to tell her? Why didn't I visit her to tell her? I had nothing to do anyway, I was down and depressed too. We could have been depressed together. Maybe then she wouldn't have killed herself.

In her note my Aunt Sara wrote that she was in too much pain to live anymore.

Too much pain to live anymore.

My aunt had fibromyalgia. It is a disease in the body that surfaces as fatigue, weakness and physical pain. Many mixed opinions can be found to argue the cause of fibromyalgia and what it links to. In my opinion, it appears to be a name of something that the doctors cannot really explain, but can only provide various medications to relieve the pain. She used those medications to relieve the pain, permanently.

And somehow I got it. Eventually it made sense. How could someone be in too much pain to smile or too much pain to sit up and then too much pain to lay down? She was in physical, mental and emotional pain and they became too much. For her the pain became overwhelming. She began focusing on the pain and it began to consume her. We can all relate to pain, can't we? Whether it is the physical, emotional or mental pain, we have all had the challenge of pain. If we focus on the pain, it can consume us too. We become totally consumed by the pain and that's all we start to see. We do not notice anything else. My Aunt Sara was consumed by the pain and the only way out for her was to end it. Her focus on the pain took over and she made a decision one day that changed the lives of everyone who knew her forever.

It certainly changed my life. I recognized that there was another way outside of focusing on the pain that we are in. Where we place our focus makes all the difference in our life. I didn't have the chance to share that with my aunt, because at the time I didn't realize I knew something so valuable about the power of focus. It was the death of my aunt that revealed it for me. It was also the death of my aunt that created a drive to determine how to support people in pain. I became willing to do whatever I could possibly do in this lifetime to get the message of peace out. Then maybe, just maybe, even if only one person gets the message and learns their way to grow out of the pain they are in, instead of remaining consumed, than it would be worth it to me. One life saved is one person who has the ability to change the world for millions. That person just doesn't know it yet because the pain is the only focus. Like a snap of your fingers, focus can be changed.

This experience with my Aunt Sara shook me up. The fear of losing someone close to me had to be faced without a choice. My Aunt Sara and I were really close. We shared the same birthday and she was the only person who was as convinced as I was that I was meant to be a star. She supported absolutely everything that I did. The card left on her table was deserved and it burned me inside to know that she never read how much I appreciated her and loved her. That was the purpose of writing the cards- to let people know before it was too late, yet it was still too late. It was too damn late and I couldn't do anything about it, except ask the question why?

Many of us who were affected by my Aunt Sara's death asked the question why? The whole experience became like an investigation. Was this planned? How long was it planned? Did someone else know about it? How did it get to this point? Many questions were asked over and over and over again. Suddenly I realized we were in a rat wheel, running and running and getting absolutely nowhere. We were stuck in the question why? Our mind is magnificent, when we ask a question, it will seek and seek until we can find an answer. This is how we can get stuck in our head. It becomes a race on a rat wheel, looking for an answer to a question that doesn't even matter in the end. Dead end questions give dead end answers. We cannot drive through a dead end. We have to turn around and find another way. That doesn't mean we shouldn't ask questions, it means we need to ask the right questions. I began asking different questions. How can I learn from this experience? What can I take from my relationship with my Aunt Sara and continue to nourish it and share it with others? What did I learn from my Aunt Sara as a person and from her life and how can I use that to allow her spirit to live on? I can learn from her mistakes and I can learn from what she did best. We can all do the same when we lose someone close or when we are in a position of sheer pain. We can begin to ask the right questions in order to turn us around from a dead end and find another way.

I was in the midst of my greatest fear, yet somehow I was tough and strong. It didn't feel like shock or denial. It was pretty damn real to me. Somehow, from somewhere, I had the strength to talk to the police, to tell other family members, to wait patiently as they removed the body, to hug people as they mourned, to help organize a funeral, that in her note she requested not to have. I had the strength to speak about her, the glorious woman that she was and the stubborn, pain in the neck woman that she also was. Somehow, from somewhere, I had the strength to push through. I wish I could take credit, but I believe it was divine grace.

That year, my Aunt Sara was number four of the people I had to say 'goodbye-see-you-later-talk-to-you-soon' to. I attended a funeral, one person a month, for nine months. Those nine months at a funeral home was like giving birth to becoming a rock to death. That year was about understanding death. It was about learning to accept that death is a law of the universe. Everything comes to an end, including this physical life. That is why we must honour the time we have, the people in our lives and the moments we are in, because our life is just a moment of time. Oddly enough, I know exactly how I want my own funeral to be and what I want my death to be about. I think it's natural to think about your own death when someone else dies. I had quite a bit of time to do that. Death never scared me. I have always been okay to die. I attempt to live my whole life as if it were my last day because we just never know. I am content with what happens with my life. I never feared my own death. I feared everyone else's death, but it didn't matter which of the two, I needed to learn about the lesson of impermanence. Nothing lives forever. Just as the sun rises and sets to begin and to conclude the day, a time will come for the sun to set for each of our lives. The sun has set for me having fear or anger around impermanence. I believe that there is something greater than this body. This body is just a tool to use in this life but we are part of something greater. I call it God, sometimes I say universe, grace, light or the divine. I don't really think it matters. Some call it Allah, Buddha or Nirvana, Wu Chi, Brahman; the sun, the earth the creator. To me it is just a word, depending on culture or ritual that names our source. It has been expressed many times that human beings need to have something to believe in. The human mind must believe in something else in order to survive and make sense of this thing called life. I think in my life I have experienced too many miracles and bless-ings to even wonder if something greater exists or not. It's not even an option for me. And, as far as I am concerned, if I am wrong, I could care less, because believing in something else is what has gotten me through some of the worst and best experiences of my life. Being tough and strong doesn't come from muscles, but it sure shows up when it's needed. It comes from the divine grace. We get the strength to push through difficult challenges from that grace.

The Departure

Fear, regret, grief, depression, and misery, how do we cope with these things when we are in the midst of the most tragic or difficult experiences? Fear was never really an issue for me. If I felt scared of something I made sure I did it just to face the fear– jumping out of planes, white water rafting, climbing the highest of heights, public speaking, walking on fire, touching bugs, sitting in the dark, it didn't matter. If I felt the slightest bit of fear, that was drive enough for me to face it and do whatever it was that was terrifying me. But, when it comes to death, we don't get to choose when we face that fear, it chooses us and we can choose how to respond.

At the time of my Aunt Sara's death, I ended up coping by getting busy. I got involved in absolutely everything I could possibly get involved in. After my trip to Haiti, I realized that the way some people are living in our world is completely unjust. I decided that I was going to be someone who did something to better the world instead of sit back and complain about how unjust and corrupt it is. That's what I focused on. I started working again at the Community Girls' Home; I began working for an international development organization doing work in Haiti; I volunteered for a distress line and got suicide ASSIST training; I worked at a community home for adults with physical and mental disabilities; I volunteered at a hospice; I did talks in schools and inspired young people to get involved; I served people food in a restaurant; and I started my own energy counseling practice. Wow, I never really listed it all out like this before. I sound like I went crazy that year. What really happened during that time was I found myself in contributing to others. I never did end up doing the Au Pair thing. I questioned why would I go somewhere else to live with another family and take care of the kids of someone else when I have a family and kids in my life to take care of at home? That did not mean I let go of my love for traveling, I still travelled, it just meant that my "family" became more than my immediate family tribe. My community and my globe were now family too. I realized I didn't need to go to LA or New York for that.

My fear, my regret and my pain pushed me into a massive response to support the people around me. I pushed through my grief by supporting others. I refused to let it hold me back, but instead it brought me to who I am. Fear is a little bit like that. Once we can name what we

Page | 43

are scared of, we can take time to determine what it is linked to and why it has become a fear in the first place. Then, we can determine how to use that fear to push us forward instead of holding us down. That's the difference between people who want to travel and do it and people who want to travel and never do. We can always find reasons not to do something, but it takes creativity and the will to find reasons to do something. We can look to the pain to hold us back or we can look to the joy that brings us forward. The truth is, life is not filled with fear or regret, only an opportunity for lessons and learning. Regret only comes when are you are not focusing on the lesson, which in hindsight is always a gift.

Imagine what your life would be like if you chose to look at the pain, the fear and the regret; what would that look like for you? What would that look like if you stayed in that place for the next year, or the next ten years? Where would you be?

Imagine what your life would look like if you chose to learn how to push through to the feeling of joy and follow your dreams to live out the life that you desire. Imagine having a life filled of passion to enjoy and to share with others through contributing to the world. How could you use your experiences of challenge or pain to grow through and to share with others? What would that look like? What would that look like right now, in this moment if you chose to live it? How would that look down the road if you decided to focus on your joy and desires, right now, in this moment?

For me, that moment looked like writing a book. So I did. For you, well, only you can determine it; I recommend a departure out of a world of fear and into a life you love. It's so worth it.

Eagle Exercise

*Take a moment to write a list of four things you have alway
ed to do. What has stopped you from taking action to make those things happen?
What fears are linked to the things on your list? What is holding you back? What
joy would come if you were to complete your list? What has become more important for
you, the fear or the joy? Right now, in this moment, schedule to do something this
week that you have always wanted to do and never did. If you accomplish that, do
something else next week. Then celebrate.*

THE JOURNAL

Some people may argue that a journal is the most important item you bring on a trip. It could be a fair tossup between journal, camera and underwear. Although underwear may seem important, a way to record the trip tends to be at the top of the list. For me, I always thought the journal was the most important. In fact, that was the case on a particular trip I took to Spain. My friend David and I decided to complete the Camino de Santiago. This is a pilgrimage walk that typically begins in St Jean Pied de Port in France and continues across northern Spain to Santiago. We both were planning to do the walk together and then continue our travels separately afterwards. This made packing for the trip a bit tricky because what was needed for the walk was much less than what was needed for the other traveling we planned to do. David convinced me that it didn't matter what we brought because everything in our bag would only make us stronger. The first day of walking all I could hear were those words from David and I thought for sure that day I was going to hit him. However, it was still my choice what I packed for that trip and it was also my choice to welcome the lesson of separating from material things. We didn't just hike through the country, we decided to do it pilgrim style. This meant no cell phone, no phone, no IPod, no computer, in addition to no razors, no products, and supposed-ly no problems for one month. We wanted to completely experience what a pilgrimage felt like. I think all I really had was soap, clothes and shoes. We did have shampoo but forgot it in a shower along the way. I told myself that I didn't need anything except for my journal. As attached as I am to my camera and to taking photos, the journal became more important. I figured I can always buy a new camera, but I could not buy thoughts and experiences.

Day one we hiked up a mountain. Day two we walked 40 kilometers in the wrong direction. Day three we walked 40 kilometers in the correct direction. Day three, that was the day we arrived at the next albergue (which is a pilgrim hostel) and that is the day I realized that I had left my journal under the pillow at the last place we stayed. I was frantic. I asked the lady running the albergue to contact the other albergue in hopes that it would be there. She could not get in contact with anyone but shared with me that if I chose to take a taxi back it would be one Euro for every kilometer. It would cost me 80 Euro to get my journal back. David, in his compassionate, understanding and frank way told me to forget about it. I knew he was right. I was so upset and frustrated with myself; I could not believe I left behind the single most important thing to me, my journal! So what do you do when you have walked all day and have become totally upset about something? Well, I went for a walk!

I stomped around for a bit. I cried. I was mad at myself in my head. Why would I put it under my pillow? What was I thinking? I got on a rat wheel, but eventually I stopped beating myself up over it. It was done. I clearly wasn't going to go back to get it. That decision in itself obviously demonstrated that it wasn't worth 80 Euro, even though I thought it was priceless. The real point was acceptance. I needed to accept that it was gone. I needed to accept that it was okay it was gone. Maybe someone else's eyes had to see those words for a reason. Maybe the words I wrote were going to offer support to another pilgrim. I was okay with that idea. Finally, I sat in silence. I noticed the sun setting behind the houses in the distance. I sat with my breath and calmed down. I realized this was exactly the lesson that I needed to experience in order to really detach from material things. I had to understand that the meaning and importance I held for my journal, being the single most important thing in my life, clearly was not accurate. I just survived walking 40 kilometers. I was safe. I was healthy. I was strong. Was forgetting my journal behind really the most important thing in the world? Was it really the worst thing that could have possibly happened? The answer is no and more often than not, when we replace the word journal with almost anything, the answer is no. I gave myself the space to cry it out and be mad, but then I focused on the things I had to be grateful for that day and just as the sun set, I let it go.

For me the whole pilgrimage was about peeling off layers and realizing what is truly important. As it turns out it wasn't my face cream, shampoo or, most shocking, not even my journal. The physical world is only a mixture of elements we can use and enjoy for periods of time. The material world does not define us as individuals or as human beings. Most goods are not things that we absolutely need to survive. At some point we put emphasis and meaning on things that we hold with such truth. We define it as something and we allow it to become who we are. Peeling those layers off allows you to discover who you really are. Who you are is not something you own.

We put meaning on items and material things. The meanings attached to these things can develop the belief that they are of greater importance than everything else. Many times I have encountered someone with literally nothing, but they are so happy even though they do not have a thing. This begs to question, if someone has nothing, what makes that person so happy? Yet, next to that person can be someone with everything, who is completely unhappy. Humans are fascinating to me.

We do not need to turn to material items to bring our happiness. Everything we need we already have. Everything else is just a tool or a toy. Again we are programmed to think we need something outside of us to bring us happiness. I grew up in a society that creates a belief that we need a medication to "fix" everything. Those who do not believe in using medication to "fix" everything then rely on "retail therapy" to create happiness (the act of purchasing something to make things all better). We do not need certain products to become better people. Happiness comes from within. The way we choose to see the world and the way we choose to be in the world is up to us and that determines our happiness.

I didn't need my journal to have a significant experience, although I wanted my journal in order to record the significant experience. Recording my experiences in some way is also why I take photos on my trips. I take all these photos and write down all these thoughts, ideas, feelings and experiences, yet, to be honest I don't think my family has even seen the photos from my very first trip to Italy. I know that no one reads my journals. Not only do we not need these material possessions, but also, the material possessions actually pull us away from the experiences we are so desperately trying to record! Some people return home to view their photos and then they experience the exact trip over again because their eyes were hiding behind the lens the entire trip. They might as well have googled their destination and saved a couple thousand dollars. I have noticed it is very rare to accurately capture the moment from traveling on a camera, not impossible, but very rare. When you are truly experiencing your journey you are soaking in the sounds, the smells, the sights, the colours, the people, and the feelings. Trying to do that in a photograph or in writing requires time, effort, creativity and focus. When your time, effort, creativity, and focus are on capturing the moment, it is not on being in the moment. I witness this all the time with parents trying to capture the moments of their children, but it takes them away from actually being part of that moment.

Being present and in the moment is one of the most significant gifts you can give to yourself no matter where you are or what you are doing. It is also one of the most significant gifts you can give to someone else. We live in a culture of distractions and receiving someone's undivided attention is rare. Most people don't even give that attention to their own children then they wonder why their kids get into trouble or do not listen. When we do not model listening, we really should not expect it. Listening means really engaging in what a person is sharing with you; paying attention to the way they are speaking and to their body language; and demonstrating with your own body language that you are listening and engaged. This means putting the phone away, shutting off the television, maintaining eye contact, and sincerely demonstrating a genuine concern about what the person is saying to you. Listening also means putting aside your own thoughts, ideas and input of the conversation and providing the time and space for someone else to share their thoughts, ideas and input. It is not a time to think about all the things you have to do or where else you should be or how you disagree with what is being said. It means being present with the person you are with, honouring them by fully engaging your ears and deactivating your busy mind.

Listening is magical. It allows you to connect, to understand and to relate to another person. It is one of the simplest things we can do, yet it has become one of the most difficult things for people to learn. We are bombarded with so much pollution of sound and distraction that listening has become a rare trait. Listening is really mastering being in the moment. Have you found at times reading parts of this book you have zoned out and had no idea what you read and had to go back to the top of the paragraph to re-read it again? I'd like to think it has nothing to do with my writing and everything to do with the fact that we tend to zone out of the moment we are in. If you just did it now, clearly this paragraph is important for you to grasp.

Some of us are so outside of the moment that we are in, all we focus on is the past experiences that have already occurred or the future experiences that have yet to happen. Life has become go, go, go and moments pass us by one after another without us even being part of them. Developing a mindfulness of the moment that we are in allows us to fully enjoy each moment as we are in it. We can go and do and see everywhere in the world, but when we are not there to enjoy it, why bother? Not being in the moment that we are in is a clear indicator that we are stuck somewhere else. Sometimes we get stuck with an event, a relationship or a situation that has already occurred. We review it over and over and over again, each time attempting to determine another way to have experienced it differently. Perhaps we are reviewing another thing to have said or to have done differently. This is the birth of regret. Regret can hold us back in the past or regret can push us to live a life we don't mind living over again when we share the stories or remember the memories. Sometimes getting stuck in the past is to escape the present that we are not content being in. We look to the past for that fulfillment instead of looking at the present moment and determining what can be done to feel fulfilled, now.

Getting stuck in the future can also take us out of the present moment. Thinking and thinking and thinking about a situation or event that has not even occurred can develop anxiety or worry. It creates stress and for no reason. That which has not happened yet is still in our control to determine how it unfolds. If we focus on worry, anxiety, stress and fear, we generate that energy and likely will generate the experience that reflects that energy as well. Worry is like a swing, it gives you something to do, but it doesn't get you anywhere. As you are thinking, worrying and stressing over the next thing to come, you are completely missing out on the moment you are in; in fact you are creating the moment you are in to be a stressful one.

Learning to be in the moment you are in will reduce stress. This is why meditation has become so popular in stress reduction. Although there are many types of meditations, typically meditation is about checking in with yourself in the moment and allowing yourself the time and space for your mind to be where your physical body is. It is developing a skill to quiet the busy mind talk that always seems to be occurring. For some people this may seem impossible. For me, it is possible and if I can manage to quiet my mind, I am convinced anyone can learn how too! Meditation is a tool to learn mindfulness. Mindfulness is a state of being. Being mindful means being mindful of your thoughts, your words, your actions, your environment, your interactions, your conversations, your experiences, your feelings and, in short, being mindful of you. Mindfulness is noticing without judging, just noticing.

Practicing mindfulness can begin by noticing your environment. Tune into your senses. Notice what you see. Notice what you smell. Notice what you can hear. Sitting in nature is one of the best places to practice this. Many people feel calm and at peace in nature. This occurs because nature has an influence on bringing you into the moment and developing a connection in that moment. Practicing mindfulness can also begin with the food you eat. Look at your food. Notice the colours, the textures, and the shapes. When you put food in your mouth, taste it, feel those textures, notice the sensations and the taste buds that are activated. Can you relate to eating your food in this way? Most people barely chew their food, let alone taste it. Many people eat on the go or eat while they are doing something else, such as watching television or engaging in conversation. Before we know it the plate is empty and we barely notice if we are still hungry or not before finishing a dessert or snack. As it turns out, when we attempt to chew our food it actually tastes better, we don't end up eating as much, and it also helps with our digestion. Why not eat mindfully?

Becoming mindful is providing yourself with a gift to notice the beauty that is constantly surrounding you. It allows you to take control of the time you have in life and not constantly feel like you do not have enough time. Really all you have is time. Everyone has the exact same amount of time every day, 24 hours. The choice is yours on what you decide to spend your time doing. Are you watching your life through a lens? Or, are you at home looking at someone else's pictures? Are you looking at your own pictures over and over again? Or are you the one in front of the camera, living in a moment that is worth taking a photo of? Whatever story you have been living in you can always begin a new chapter. Your life is your journal and you are the author. When you look back and read it over, the joy and happiness can be shared all over again. When you live in each moment and are mindful of how you live your life, your story becomes more fulfilling. Life is more than the journal, the camera and the underwear; life is about the moments you are trying to capture and just like the underwear inside your clothing, the happiness can be found on the inside of you. As Ralph Waldo Emerson shared, 'though we travel the world over to find the beautiful, we must carry it with us or we would find it not.' Developing mindfulness has nothing to do with material possessions and everything to do with what you already are, what you already have, and everything else can only make those better. You can notice who you are and what surrounds you, and you can practice not only mindfulness, but also gratitude.

Eagle Exercise

In your own journal, take a moment to list the things in your life that you have made important. What do you have that you feel you could not live without? From that list circle the things that are top on the list. Test yourself, can you go a day without that one thing? Or an even greater challenge of going a weekend or a week without it? Try it, I dare you.

This week begin to notice when you are in the moment and when you have zoned out. Just for today, completely practice mindfulness while you eat a meal. Notice the food before you eat. Notice the temperature, colours, textures, and shapes. When it is in your mouth, notice the tastes, experience the sensations. Chew the food. Take your time and practice mindfulness while you are eating. If you notice a difference, choose a meal again tomorrow to begin your practice of mindfulness.

THE JOURNEY

Traveling is not about where you are going; traveling is about how you end up at your destination. Many hostel walls display the quote, 'Life is a journey not a destination.' When we only look to the destination, we miss everything else including significant magic moments along the way.

I was in Arequipa, Peru, traveling with two great friends, Sean and Lindsay. I had in my head that I wanted to go to Museo Santuarios Andinos. It is a museum in the town that had a display of Momia Juanita, which is the Inca Ice Maiden. It is a well-preserved frozen body of an Inca girl from the 1400s who was discovered in 1995 on the Andes cordillera in southern Peru. It was stuck in my head that I wanted to see this display and I wanted to get there before the museum closed for the day. Because it had an early closing time, I was mindful of the time.

All morning things were going slow, from getting up, to getting food, to making food, and finally to getting on our way. I was getting a bit eager to get to the museum on time before it closed. While walking there we passed by dozens of places that offered different excursions. It wasn't till the end of the plaza when Sean mentioned that we should go into the last shop to check for white water rafting excursions. Reluctantly I agreed because we were planning to go on a raft excursion the next day and had yet to set it up. Lindsay and I were speaking to the lady about different options and were about to make a decision, but Sean had disappeared. Finally, he returned with his big smile. He shared with us that he met a man who invited us to go to the roof of the building and check out the entire plaza from the top. Lindsay and I were half interested, as we were trying to sort out the rafting excursion. We updated Sean, decided on a package and paid for the trip. As we walked outside, Sean asked if we wanted to go. At this point, I completely forgot what he was talking about and he had to remind us that he met this man. As it turns out, Sean had to go to the bathroom and went next door, upstairs to a restaurant. The owner of the restaurant told him he could climb to the top of the roof for one of the best views in Arequipa. Sean mentioned he was with friends and the man told him to return with his friends.

The three of us climbed up the dark, narrow staircase and down an old, compact hallway. The man was working on an addition above the restaurant and the first thing he said to us was, "Welcome home!" I was perplexed by his choice of greeting and wondered how he knew we felt at home in Peru. He pointed us in the direction to continue to the top of the roof and said to take our time, take as many photos as we wanted, and then he would explain. We weren't exactly sure what he was going to explain, but we were excited to head to the top of the roof. We climbed a couple of ladders to a flat roof and walked to the edge, looking down to the plaza. In the distance were gorgeous sites of architecture, people, and of course, the volcano tops in the distance. It was beautiful. Time appeared to stop while we were up there and it seemed as though our only interest was having a photo shoot with the three of us. When we finished, we climbed back down to meet the man on the main floor. Our new friend, Walter, invited us in the kitchen and began to show us all of the ancient dishes they serve traditional Peruvian food in, all made of clay. He began speaking to us about languages. He would say one word in English then say another word in a different language to connect the actual word itself and the meaning. He connected English words to Spanish, German, French, Latin, and Chinese. He demonstrated through the words how all the languages were connected, even though we see them as separate. He spoke with such wisdom about languages and culture and elegantly connected the languages together.

When he finished he said, "You see, we are all connected, we are all one, therefore, welcome home!"

Walter brought us out to the dining area on the terrace. We sat down and listened to Walter share knowledge about culture, people and history. He told us his knowledge was not intelligence it was that he had a big heart! He spoke about the energy of the body, healing, and how we are connected to the earth. He even pulled out a map and showed us all of the places we needed to see in Arequipa. He told us about the energy vortexes of the earth in the area and explained how everything relates to the energy areas of the earth. He said there were no such thing as coincidences and that everything was planned and happening for a reason. He told us to jump into a taxi to check out the lost pyramids. I asked him if he would come with us. Clearly by this point, I had scrapped the museum idea. He looked at me with a smirk, debating the invitation, yet seemingly knowing that he would be joining us. He said he had to finish a few things in the kitchen and afterwards he would come with us.

The day took a twist. We ended up having a personal tour of the entire area, visiting incredible energy vortexes of the earth, as well as visiting Inca ruins you would never find in a travel guide. We learned about the history of the land and the people. The three of us were consistently blown away, speechlessly looking at each other sharing huge smiles of walking into this experience. That night we returned to Walter's restaurant and had a huge meal of traditional Peruvian food with imported wine from across the globe. We laughed, we talked, we ate, we drank and we learned. We learned quite a bit that night. Among many things, we learned that sometimes the destination is not what you think it is going to be. We learned to be grateful within the journey.

Walter shared a toast that night that I will carry with me for life. He stood up beside the balcony as we sat at the table looking up at him. Each time he mentioned a thank you, he poured a bit of his drink over the balcony to touch Pachamama, which means Mother Earth. With each drop to Pachemama, he said: Thank you to Pachamama, without her we are nothing. She gives us the fruit and the food that we need. Thank you to the mountain angel, who is among all things and consistently watching over us. Thank you to the oceans and to the winds, as they are the energy of the universe. Thank you to our parents, without them we would not exist in being here. Thank you to our sons and to our daughters, as they are our future. Thank you to our brothers and our sisters as they walk down the path of life with us. Thank you to those who love, as love makes the world go round. Thank you to Pachamama.

Walter shared with us, what I would like to share with you. We do not experience accidents, just experiences. Life is just lessons and learning. Everyone chooses his/her life and now we can choose our own. We can choose to be grateful for our experiences, as each of them brought us to this moment.

I look back to this experience and I wonder, what would have happened if life was about the destination for me that day and I just went to the museum? I would have missed this entire magical experience. Walter told us that "ma" means "mother" and "gic" means father, making "magic" a balance of mother and father earth energy. This is a balance of masculine and feminine energy. Everything is made up of energy, including our own being. Energy follows our thoughts and our words. When we are aware of our own energy, we can become aware of the universal energy we are connected to. Universal energy is like the magic of that day. Is it a coincidence that Sean had to go to the bathroom at that particular moment and decided on that particular restaurant? We walked by dozens of places we could have booked a rafting excursion, but we stopped when we did. I was stuck on going to the museum, but eventually I had to surrender to the flow we were part of and allow the magic to occur. I could have easily gotten upset with Sean for the detour, but instead we all went with it. Was it just a coincidence that the man we met that day was filled with wisdom and knowledge about life and lesson that we needed to hear about? We spent many conversations discussing many similar ideas that Walter brought to our attention. He took it to another level for us. The magic of that day was part of the universal flow. A coincidence is a co incident, meaning incidents occurring together. It can be considered synchronicity. We can place what meaning we want on these incidents as we notice them, but that day was filled with them and I could only be grateful for the magic moments that occurred one after another. The flow of the journey took my focus off the destination; however, it provided me with information and memories that will be part of my life forever. I am forever thankful for the magic of that experience and the magic of my every day.

Noticing magic and allowing magic to be part of your life is about being part of the natural flow of the universe. This means learning to dance within your experiences and let life happen with you, not to you. We create this magic and it doesn't happen with getting stuck on a destination and it sure as hell doesn't happen with getting stuck in the past. Our past experiences do not define who we are. We define who we are right now and in this moment. We choose who to be by demonstrating who we are being right now and in this moment. When we are open to experience the journey and open to being part of the "flow" we begin to notice that each step of the way is in fact guided for us. People, signs, messages are constantly being provided to support our highest good, our desires and our dreams. It is our birthright to be happy and the universe supports our joy.

These are big ideas, especially when these ideas are new to you. It may seem like a load of spiritual fluff, however, magic is in the eye of the believer. We do not need to call this God or Buddha or Disney. You can choose what to believe, but the idea is to choose things to believe that are going to empower you, wake you up and allow you to be you and not a sheep in society, in the middle of the heard, blinded by the wool of those around you, hoping to get to a destination. You can choose to move through life, stopping when you are told to stop, sitting when you are told sit, eating what you are told to eat, drinking what you are told to drink and believing what you are told to believe. You choose to believe that you are worthless, you are not good enough, you are wrong, you can't do that, you should do this, and you need to be this way! Know that people in your life who are telling you what to do, usually tell you this from a place of care, concern and love. They share what they know at the time they know it and they give the best they have. Those people are also people who were told all of the same messages. This has nothing to do with those people and everything to do with you. It is about you taking responsibility of your life and who you are meant to be. Life is magic! It is beautiful, fun and exciting! Life does involve pain, hurt and disappointment; however, you can choose how to respond to the experiences that are difficult and challenging. You can let those experiences define you or you can let those experiences provide you with the lessons you need to grow. Suffering is a choice and so is living.

When we choose to experience the journey towards whatever destination we are heading towards, we choose to live life with gratitude. Life moves out of being a series of disappointments and into a series of blessings. I wasn't disappointed I didn't go to the museum, I was grateful. No matter where you are or what you have experienced, this movement can happen right now. It begins with gratitude. Take time to notice the things to be thankful for. Understand your life within the bigger picture. In any situation there are things to be thankful for. It is like a storm. The clouds come in, and it pours and pours and pours rain. The vicious winds come soaring through. It is dark, wet and seemingly hopeless. Yet, above it all, the sky is still blue and the sun is still shining. It always is, even as it storms. It appears wet and gloomy, but you know the sun is there, above the dark clouds somewhere shining bright.

When you live life looking to the sun, you will always know which direction to go. First of all, you know the direction because the sun always rises in the East and sets in the West, from there you will know North and South. But, secondly, to see the sun rise, you must be part of one of the most magical moments of the day, a time of silence, peace and serenity. It is the time before chaos wakes up and the mind becomes busy. The sunrise provides an opportunity to be thankful for the day and to step into your life. The sunset is one that always brings people to stop and to ponder or to reflect on the day, to capture the moment and again, an opportunity to be grateful for your experiences, even just for that day. Look to the sun and be grateful for another day and this moment.

When you look to the sun, you will always know which direction to go on your journey because you are looking to the blessings and not to the storm. In this, only more blessings will generate. Seek and you shall find. Look to the good in your life and see more good become part of your life. In the middle of darkness, a match can be lit and all the focus will go to that light. Walking through a dark room, our natural instinct is to seek out the light. We must tune into our natural instinct and seek out the light in our lives. When we explore the bricks in our luggage, face our fears, and uncover who we are, we uncover our own light. We beam in happiness, joy and love. We shine light in our lives and we share that light with others. As previously mentioned, we become the candle in a dark room. We may encounter another candle with an unlit wick. We can light that second candle just by being who we are meant to be. We make an impact on that candle and they become lit too. That candle lights up in the darkness and encounters another candle with an unlit wick. Eventually the candles create light for other candles to notice and connect wicks. From there, enough light shines and the light switch to the room can be found. The room is lit. This is called world peace. We can create peace in our world by uncovering the peace within ourselves. When we become fully who we are meant to be, we become a shining light. We encourage and influence others to shine as well. Sometimes the winds of the storm will blow out our wick. It happens. Thankfully, there are other candles that we surround ourselves with so we can connect wicks and shine again. When everyone shines, the switch can be found and eventually there is only a beautifully lit room. Light in a dark room will always and instantly become the focus naturally. However, darkness can never come into a room lit up in light and make any impact whatsoever. This is that choice mentioned before, choose love or choose fear.

This all begins on your focus. Are you choosing to focus on the light to lead you through your journey? Or are you walking blindly through the darkness? This is the journey; this is your life. You co-create the magic in your life. You choose your own adventure! Notice the magic in your life and be grateful! This is a repeated message, but it is important to know that it begins right now, in this moment, not when you get to the destination. Magic is surrounding you on your journey, waiting for you to notice and to be grateful. Each step along the way offers magic, not just the final destination.

Eagle Exercise

Spend three minutes writing a list of everything you are thankful for. When you are done, close your eyes and experience the feeling of gratitude in your body. Think of each thing you wrote on your list and imagine the feeling of gratitude filling up your heart. Allow your gratitude to increase with each inhalation you breathe in and each exhalation your breathe out. Feel the gratitude fill you up and sit with that feeling, even just for one minute. To create more happiness in your life, notice everything you can be thankful for. As you notice and focus on the things to be thankful for, more things to be thankful for will generate. Try again tomorrow.

THE STRANGERS

When I was a child, my beautiful mother would constantly drill the message, 'do not talk to strangers'. This is a common message for many of us, and rightfully so, our parents want to protect us. No one wants a child to be hurt or abducted; only those who still remain a wounded child within do that. My lovely, compassionate and caring mother would sit me down and say, "Okay Laura, now if a stranger walks up to you and says, 'hello little girl, I have some candy, would you like one?'" and let me assure you, she would deepen her voice and act out the creepy image she had in her head of a person who would steal children. Then she would continue with, "What would you say?"

Innocently and happily, I would answer, "Yes!"

"NO," my mother would grab me by the shoulders and shout at the top of her lungs, "No Laura! You do not talk to strangers! I don't care what they have for you, Laura! You do not take it! Do you understand?"

Of course I would tell her yes. As I understood it, you never take anything from strangers. She would be relieved and continue her Mama Rosa Training. "Okay, so if you are outside the grocery store waiting for me and a man tells you that he has a box of puppies in his car, would you go look at the puppies?"

Innocently and happily, I would answer, "Yes!"

"NO," my mother would grab me by the shoulders and shout at the top of her lungs, "No Laura! You do not talk to strangers! I don't care what they have to give you or what they have to show you! Do you understand?"

Of course I would tell her yes. As I understood it, you never take anything from strangers and you never look at anything they want to show you. She would be relieved and continue her Mama Rosa Training. "Okay, so now, imagine you are at the park and an old lady falls to the ground, do you go help her?"

Innocently and happily, I would answer, "Yes!"

"NO," my mother would grab me by the shoulders and shout at the top of her lungs, "No Laura! You do not talk to strangers! I don't care what they have to give you or to show you or if they need help! You go get someone you know! You do not talk to strangers! Do you understand?"

Innocently and happily, I would answer, "yes!"

By this point my mother was not convinced. In fact, she drilled it into me so much that I wasn't even allowed to trust people that I did know! If someone, other than my Mom or Dad came to pick me up from school, they would need to know the "secret password". One day, my Aunt Lisa came to pick me after school because something came up and my Mom couldn't. I would not leave with her because she couldn't remember the password. At this point, you must think I have trust issues with the world. You would think.

As important as I believe it is to inform children and make them aware of what is safe and what is unsafe, talking to strangers in my life has created some of the most significant experiences for me. That does not mean I am not cautious, I assure you (mom) I am. I feel as though I have family in every country I've visited, simply because I look at the world as my home and everyone in it becomes family. When I was in Chile, I was sitting on a bus traveling from one city to the next. I was sitting next to a larger, older, Chilean man. I have a blessed ability to sleep anywhere and sitting on a long bus ride is great way to knock me out for hours. That is exactly what I did, however, as soon as this man saw my eyes open, he was quick to start talking to me. He talked and talked and I listened and I laughed. He was speaking Spanish and at the time, I knew only the word, "Hola!" He didn't care. Oddly enough, somehow we communicated quite well and I picked up words here and there to put them together to make sense of what he was trying to say. Once he found out I was Italian, we managed to speak broken English, broken Italian and broken Spanish. He told me his daughter could speak English, so he called her on the phone. I thought he called her to translate something he wanted to tell me. Instead, he ended up just calling her, while I sat next to him, to tell her that he met someone who spoke English! It was priceless.

What was really helpful was the fact that once he heard what city we were planning to stop in, he informed us it was a bad idea because the city was unsafe. He started conversations with other locals to confirm his opinion. They agreed. He told us to stop in his city because it was beautiful. So, on this journey, we shifted destinations. We got off at his stop and he told us to wait with him so we could meet his family. So we did. I was watching for cars passing by, but after some time, two older women and two younger women were coming our way, pushing a shopping cart, also priceless. The man introduced us to his family, shoved all of his things in the cart and invited us to join him. So we did.

That night we had dinner with the family, indulged in classic Gato Negro vino, and used Google Translator online to communicate with one another. We sang and danced and laughed. The family consisted of the Father, Mother and two daughters, and the eldest daughter's boyfriend with their two boys. All of them made that night one never to forget. In the wee hours of the morning, together, they walked us to our hostel. All ten of us were walking down the middle of the road, laughing and carrying on joyfully. In the morning Papa was there to wake us up and take us for another adventure! He brought us back to their house and the entire family was walking in and out of the house filling up the back of a pickup truck. I think they emptied their house and put it in the truck. Table, chairs, blankets, bags, food, the dog, and eventually the Canadians along with the whole family got into that truck. The night before they asked if we wanted to go swimming with them the next day and we agreed, but this appeared to be a moving day!

We drove for some time off a main road and onto dirt paths. We were surround by trees and drove around a couple of cows. In and out of potholes, we stopped at a small stream. A couple of the kids jumped out, checked it out and whatever they were looking for this area didn't have it. They jumped back in and we continued deeper into the forested area. Finally we stopped again and everybody got out. On a dirt road, beside a river, in the middle of a forest, was apparently the perfect place for a picnic. The kids took off to swim in a pool created with a dam made out of garbage and the adults started pulling everything off the truck to start cooking. Papa had a huge container of a blend of different fish that he went around spoon-feeding everyone with. I can't exactly say, as a vegetarian, that I was a fan. A classic moment was when I had just made the perfect sandwich of fresh vegetables and sauce, topped with seasonings and the boyfriend came around and slapped a fish right on top that he had cooked on the fire. I was grateful, but Sean ended up eating the fish!

We spent hours at this picnic spot. Everyone ate, drank, talked and laughed. No one really spoke English fluently and we could barely speak broken Spanish, yet, somehow it worked. The love and fun we all shared that day was most memorable. Later we went to the beach to swim and to play soccer in the sand. By the end of the day everyone was exhausted and Papa was down right drunk! The next day we had another short visit before departing on our way. Saying our farewells was sad, but now I can share that I have family in Chile.

Stories like this one do not seem to faze my mother anymore. I wonder if she just expects these types of experiences to happen to me now. It seems everywhere I go I make new friends and everywhere I leave, I feel as though I leave family behind. It truly is a blessing. I am overjoyed for crossing paths with so many beautiful people. All of these people, at some point, were strangers to me. We are all strangers to each other to start. At some point we must really consider looking at people as people. We are all family and we are all on the same team. We are all human beings, yet, we are part of a world where we are segregated by colour, beliefs, age, ethnicity, country and religion. We do not have to choose to live life the exact same way or even to believe the same things. We can still be different and be respectful. I was told once that we do not need to think alike to love alike. I believe that to be true. We can have understanding, compassion, and love for people who have different beliefs. Besides most faith beliefs are all saying the same thing anyway; it just looks different through language, rituals and practices. The universal language that they all share is love.

Segregation is not just a global issue. This issue trickles to the country, to the community, to the schools, to the workplaces and finally to the homes. Many people feel like strangers to each other under the same roof, with their own blood family. If people do not look at those who are the closest to them with understanding, compassion and love, how can we ever practice it globally? Building strong relationships begins in the home and it should become a number one priority. People remain stuck in their pain and suffering and they begin to share that pain and suffering with the people whom they interact. It surfaces as anger, frustration, guilt, power and control. This is the environment we raise children in. We love the people in our lives, but with conditions. I will love you when you do this. I will love you when you become this. When will we love, because we love? The sad thing is people do not even know what love looks like. In fact, if a perfect stranger does something out of the goodness of his or her heart, others do not necessarily receive it with gratitude. Instead, they receive it with suspicion. What do they want from me? Are they trying to hide something? I must have to give something in return. It is rarely received as, "Wow what a nice and thoughtful gesture! I am so grateful!" On the flip side, many times we give and give and give to the point we get pissed off that we are not receiving anything in return! When will we give limitlessly, expecting nothing in return? When we give from the heart, we are not keeping score or expecting something back. Giving from the heart is giving with love. Love fills both sides of the giving and receiving. When we give from the heart, we automatically feel filled up too.

When a stranger looks at us the wrong way, or says something a certain way, suddenly that becomes an issue. We have so many wounded children walking around in adult bodies and so much hurt covered with anger and spite. To tell people that life is precious and there is so much to be grateful for is like escaping a psychological treatment hospital in your underwear; people think you are nuts!

My philosophy is I'd rather be nuts and happy than sane and miserable. A good friend told me that it is only insane if you do not produce results. If being happy creates a remarkable life, than it's not insane. What is truly insane is that not enough people are trying it. Instead people mask pain with medications or material possessions. People go around treating the people they love like dirt. Sadly, most people are walking through life with their head down missing all the beauty there is to see is. To me, it's like living life dead compared to how alive it feels to find joy, peace and fulfillment. Why live life dead? That's what being dead is for. Even being dead is better than that. I try to do anything I can to encourage people to find what makes them happy and do more of it. If you don't know what that is, then keep trying different things until you figure it out. Don't settle at a point that doesn't feel fulfilling. Seek and you shall find. People ask me all the time what's my secret. The secret is I am happy. The truth is, it's not a secret, it just looks unfamiliar because too many people settle for good instead of great. I don't settle for happiness, I seek out bliss and bliss is accompanied by love.

Because each and every one of us knows what pain looks like and knows how it feels, when we encounter someone who is miserable, is it really worth being miserable too? Perhaps that person could use a little joy, even just for that moment. Instead of responding with anger, we can respond with love. Ways to practice love include small gestures like taking an extra minute to talk to someone, waiting an extra half second to hold the door for someone behind you, saying thank you and have a good day, but actually mean it, genuinely or even simply saying I love you when you feel it. This is joining the team of global citizens. It is an understanding that we are all on the same team as human beings and we need to start playing together.

Actually taking the time to sit and talk to people you live with can make the world of a difference in your world. Engage in conversations with curiosity and love, as well as offer support. Simply just listening, having a mere presence for the people in our life is usually a gift of gold. It's called take a step off the rat wheel for once and stop the go, go, go that you think there is no choice to be part of. You have a choice. What and who is important to you? Connect with people and build relationships. Relationships help to uncover who we are and they support others to become who they are as well. Sometimes we are the one who needs to take the first step in repairing our relationships. Who are we being in that relationship? If we focus on our own work in the relationship, the relationship will shift naturally. When we focus on expecting it to be the other person's responsibility to fix this relationship, then expect to keep waiting. You must remember this is your life, you are choosing what it looks like and you can choose who you are being in the relationships that you are in. What kind of son or daughter are you being? What kind of friend, boyfriend or girlfriend are you being? What kind of student or teacher are you being? What kind of parent are you being? What kind of person do you wish to be?

Strangers are people we do not know. We can be strangers to the people in our own home. We can be strangers to ourselves. Love, compassion and understanding must begin with how you see yourself. Then you can use that same love, compassion and understanding to see others around you. See people as you see yourself and live a life where no one is a stranger anymore.

Eagle Exercise

Today, contact someone you love that has become like a stranger. Call the person just to talk and to let them know you love them. Turn everything else off, sit, and engage in the conversation. Really listen to that person and give them the gift of your attention; the present of presence. Give a gift to a stranger: buy a coffee or meal for someone or wrap a gift and hand it to someone and simply say, "You look like a person who deserves a reason to smile." Try it again tomorrow.

THE GURU

I have been on the search for my Guru for years. I feel as though many people on a spiritual quest encounter a Guru- a teacher to guide them along the way. I love books, but I am not a big reader. I prefer to interact with people. In my head, I felt the best way to learn would be to find a Guru. I pictured my Guru sitting under a tree somewhere, drinking herbal tea, or perhaps in the back of some shop, in a tiny room of boxes, burning incense and meditating. The Monkette could study with a Monk somewhere in the middle of an untouched forest. That's how I saw it for a long time. In fact, when I would seek out my Guru, I would meet spiritual people and share with them that I was looking for my Guru. Countless times, I have been told, "The Guru is within."

That would stump me at first. A part of me believed that to be true because I have always felt connected to an inner wisdom that simply guided me every step of the way. I would do things that my mind would wonder if it was right or wrong, but my heart would be completely certain it was the way to go. When I began tuning into this guidance and trusting it, I was never led astray. My whole healing and energy counseling practice began in this way. Initially I heard from a friend about Reiki. As he explained it to me, it was like reminding me of something that I already knew about. In that moment, I knew I needed to find out more.

When I was in university, I had a professor who spent a whole class talking about energy work and Reiki. He let us practice on each other. The energy I was playing with was so strong and so familiar. Finally, I encountered a woman named Lynda. After talking about Reiki over and over again, my friend Kellie bought me a gift certificate to get a treatment with Lynda. Soon after that I took her classes. She taught me to become a Reiki Master, but everything I learned was like a reminder of something I already knew within.

That knowing is our inner wisdom. This inner wisdom is always part of us, no matter what age we are. Some people describe it as, 'a gut feeling' or they were just 'pushed to go that way'. For example, many people have the experience of taking the same way to work every single day, then one day they decide to turn down a different road. They later find out there was a massive accident the way they usually go. Other people have the experience of calling a friend who answers the phone and says, 'oh I was just thinking about you'. What a coincidence, right? Co-incident is the fact that two incidents are occurring in line with one another. Our inner wisdom is connecting with a message of the universe. Tuning into this allows us to be guided no matter where we are or what we are doing. Nurturing and honouring this inner wisdom, this connection, will allow us to enter into the flow of life.

When I was a child, I went down a water slide at a water park and my Mom was at the bottom waiting for me. The water from the slide entering the water of the pool created extremely rough waters. It was meant to be fun to enter the rough waters, but I was young and I couldn't swim. I was stuck underwater for a really long time. It's a shock I didn't drown. My Mom was in a panic searching for me and thankfully saw my hand rising out of the bubbly water, desperately seeking help. She grabbed me and pulled me up. I was terrified, coughing and wailing. That day I decided I was scared of water.

When I got older and started traveling, anytime I felt a fear of doing an activity, it created a desire to do the activity in order to overcome the fear. What better way to overcome the fear of water than to go white water rafting on the Nile River? So that's what I did. Mind you, I was terrified. I made sure I sat right next to the boat guide and I told him that I wasn't a strong swimmer. My stomach was in knots even though everyone was laughing and having fun. I still managed to enjoy myself. The Nile River is extremely wide and gorgeous. Surrounding it are beautiful trees, rich greenery and singing birds that create an incredible melody. This, of course, is during the times the waters are calm between extremely rough rapids. On the raft, we cruised along, taking in the scenery, listening to the birds. Every so often a fish would leap out of the water and back in again. It wasn't rare to see the odd monkey swinging in the trees or staring back at us. While traveling down the river, suddenly in the distance, the sound of crashing water would become louder and louder as the boat flowed along, getting closer and closer to the thunderous sounds. At this point, the guide would pipe up and begin to give directions as to where to paddle, how to sit, when to drop in the boat and when to hold on. In this moment, my life felt at stake and I wondered if I would survive this adventure I chose to put myself through.

I survived the first two rapids, although during one of them our boat flipped. Our guide told us to hold onto the rope if our boat flipped so we could stay together. This was a nightmare because I got stuck under the boat, holding on. I was consistently being banged down into the water by the boat. Eventually I managed to get out for underneath, but I thought to myself that most definitely did not feel safe. We survived it though and when everyone got back on the boat they cheered and laughed. This put a smile on my face, but I am sure my eyes still screamed horror. The next rapid, 'Big Brother', was meant to be the first of the worst. I decided if we flipped that I would let go so I would not get trapped under the boat again. Our guide said there was a sixty per cent chance of flipping on this one. Terrified, excited and ready to take it on, we got closer and closer. It is uneasy, floating down a calm, beautiful river, only to look ahead at an obvious drop into nothing. All I could do to prepare was listen to the crashes of water up ahead and pray to make it through.

Big Brother had a massive drop into a huge rapid. "Paddle hard! Paddle hard!" shouted the guide. The paddles crashed into the rapids frantically, hoping to make a difference. "Get down! Hold on!" he screamed.

I was crouched on the floor of the raft, holding onto the rope with one hand and onto the paddle with my other hand. The raft smashed into the drop. I felt the raft tilt to flip. Suddenly I soared out into the air, only to land in rapids waiting to die. I was under water. It was silent. The crashes above could not be heard, only felt. Simply knowing they were there, existing as real as ever made time freeze. I was waiting to surface, waiting to surface. I thought to myself, I would surface. According to nature, my body will go back up and I will catch as much air as possible before I get brought under again. I was still waiting. It was at this point where panic challenges patience and silence feels like death. I was just about ready to burst, still waiting. If screaming could occur under water I'm sure I would have been belting out cries that would be heard at the end of the Nile in Egypt. Somehow I managed to trust that I would surface. I guess I had no choice in that moment other than to trust and to be patient waiting. My body was brought to the top of the rapid. I wanted to sigh for relief, but instead I gasped for another breath of air and dropped back under as my face crashed into a new rapid. I thought about the time I was seven years old, sliding down the slide in Florida, crashing into rapid waves at the bottom, near to drowning until my hand reached out of the water for my mother to grab and save me. I threw my hands up, wishing my mother were there to save me again, wishing anyone were there to save me. I surfaced again to catch air and dropped under. I remember hearing a voice in my head reminding me to stay calm and lay back, with my feet down river to float through the rapids. I went under again. This time not long enough for me to wonder if I'll ever see the light of the sun again, I was floating. I saw another raft in the distance at the side of the river. I passed it quickly before I thought of a way to get myself over there. I looked for anyone from my raft. I looked for my guide, our boat. Nothing was in sight. I dropped back under from the force of the water. Startled by that one, I gasped for more air when I re-surfaced.

Finally, there he was. Twenty meters away, one of the guides in a safety kayak was making his way over to me. I threw my hands up in a "where-have-you-been, please-save-me" motion. He smiled. I am panicking at this point now that I know I can panic instead of using every ounce of my body to stay calm. He got closer. I grabbed onto the handle of the kayak and he paddled us through the rest of the rapids, stopping at the side of the river to wait for my team to meet us.

Safe, I looked behind me to where I came from and simply thanked God that I survived bodysurfing those rapids that look as though a boat could never manage. As it turns out, our boat never flipped. I thought the boat had flipped when I soared off, but apparently I was the only one to take the rapids on my own! They made it through, cheering that they conquered Big Brother Rapid, only to realize they had lost a member of the team. When I made it back on the raft, we piled our paddles in the centre of the boat, threw them up and cheered, "Team To-To!"

I felt like a cat when pulled from the water, wet, miserable and scared, but the Nile River taught me a valuable lesson. Remaining calm and patient during the most terrifying moment in my life is what saved my life. One of the first things they teach when you go white water rafting is the importance of laying back, with your feet forward and allowing the rapids to pull you through. When you try to swim or flap around, you endanger yourself. It uses up too much of your energy and it goes against the flow of the rapids, which pulls you more into the rapids, rather than allowing yourself to flow out of them and into the calmer waters.

Tuning into our inner wisdom is being part of the universal flow. When we are living life in a state of panic, worry, frustration or anger and we try to control things or flap around in the rapids of problems and stress, we actually use up more energy. This will keep us in the rapids. Learning to remain calm, to be patient and to tune into your inner wisdom is what will, in fact, save you from the rapids. Tuning into your inner wisdom is tuning into the coincidences of your life. When you are in the flow of the universe, you will feel the beauty of how things will smoothly work out on their own and how things will present themselves to you in such a way that guides you where to go next. The signs of life bring you into the flow of life. For example, signs tend to come in threes. First, you could be talking to someone and they mention a name of a book in the conversation. Then the next day, you see someone reading that same book. Later that week, you are at the store and notice that book is on sale. This is a sure sign that you likely should pick up that book and read it. If you don't notice, the message will keep coming up in different ways until it finally gets your attention. Sound familiar? Do you find that you continue to have the same experiences happen to you over and over again and wonder why it always happens to you? Take a step back and ask yourself, did you learn the lesson yet? It will continue in repetition until you get what you need to grow to the next step. Put your feet up, lay back, remain calm and patient and let the flow of the universe take you through the river of life.

The Guru within has always been part of me since I was a child. I consider myself lucky, however, it was my Mom and my Aunt Sara who always encouraged me to tune in to my intuition. Learning to master it was part of growing up. I'd like to think that we are all born fully tuned into our inner wisdom. It is always there but sometimes it gets buried. Our experiences or thoughts and beliefs tend to bury our connection to our inner wisdom. Sometimes we just need to understand the difference between our thoughts and our inner wisdom. Both come through as a voice in our head, but one is our mind chatter and another is our wisdom. One comes from the brain in our head the other comes from the brain in our heart. The Guru lives within our heart. When we take time to breathe, fill our heart with gratitude and love and sit in silence, we create the space to tune into our inner wisdom, our guidance, or our Guru.

Many people in life have no idea about the Guru within themselves and many people have no interest to seek a Guru outside of themselves. This is why life is set up with a series of teachers along the way to support our growth and personal wellbeing. We are all students and we are all teachers. We are learning and growing on our own, simultaneously teaching others whom we interact with. Once we realize this gift in our lives, things can become much smoother.

Everyone has a person or people in his or her life that are button pushers. We all experience button pushers. These are people who really get under our skin, who tend to piss us off or upset us. For some of us these people are the closest people to us in our lives. Our button pushers can be parents, siblings, good friends, coworkers or even acquaintances, strangers, oh, and of course a spouse, boyfriend or girlfriend. A part of us may love these people and really desire a peaceful relationship, yet there is just something they do to us that drives us crazy. Sound familiar? Perhaps you have a button pusher in your family. Perhaps you have someone in your life that you really care about and for the most part things are great, but every once in a while they do something that really upsets you. They do something to you. What they do is push a button. What we think they do is cause us to be upset. The truth is if there was no button to push, we wouldn't be upset.

Think of it this way. Imagine a glass of water– a full glass of water– there is no need to argue if it is half full or half empty when we can just add more water and everyone can be satisfied and filled with abundance. So, imagine this full glass of water. In this water you place some spoons. If the water has salt at the bottom of the glass and you use spoons to stir the water, the water will become cloudy. If there was no salt in your glass and you use the spoons to stir the water, the water would still remain clean. You are your own full glass of water. The teachers in your life are the spoons. When you have healing to do, teachers will come into your life, stir up your water and you will see it become cloudy. You may think it was the teachers who made you cloudy, however, if you had no salt, wounds or healing to focus on, the teachers could stir up your water and it would remain clean and calm.

The idea is to take time with the salt. Learn what you need to learn and learn where you need to grow. When a person pushes your buttons and causes you to be upset, take a step back and ask yourself what about that situation upset you? Why did that upset you? Our greatest button pushers can be our greatest teachers. They are the people who reveal that you have work to do. They are the people that help you to realize that you are carrying around luggage full of manure with you. When your glass becomes cloudy, take time to work through your salty manure and use it to grow, rather than to cause a stink.

Some people may never know their glass of water has salt sitting on the bottom. Some people may always look to the teachers who enter the glass as the reason for the salty water. Some people may just learn to live in salty water and make that the way it is. Other people will ask the teachers to help scoop out the salt. Some people might strain the water into a new glass; some salt will be taken out and some salt will remain in the water. People may strain the water over and over and over again, until the water is clean. Some just pour the water out, wash out the glass and pour new water in, while some people may get a whole new glass of water. As you can see, there are many ways to live with your glass of water. You have to choose what is right for you. Are you thirsty for clean water yet?

Many teachers can support you in cleaning your water. Many people may tell you how they cleaned their water and think that is how you should clean yours. The truth is there is no right or wrong way. As long as you are thirsty and as long as you are open to being in the flow, you will be guided by your own inner wisdom. The Guru within you will know which way to go and will know when you encounter a person meant to teach you something. Everyone you encounter is a Guru by the way, because everyone has a piece of information for you that you may need. You cannot study life in a textbook. School serves a purpose and allows you to learn about many things, but it does not teach you how to live your life. That is a choice for you to make. Everyone around you is there to support you. If you feel like someone is not supporting you, then reflect on why you feel that way. Reflect and ask the right questions that uncover answers to bring insight, knowledge and support. Why is that person pushing your buttons in feeling unsupported? What lessons do you need to learn? Do you need to learn how to stand up for what you believe in? Do you need to learn how to stand up for yourself? Is there a deep wound to heal? What do you need to heal this wound?

When you feel something, get curious and explore why you feel that way. Get thirsty for clean water. Practice patience and be calm as you allow yourself to flow downstream, rather than paddle upstream. Wasting energy going upstream is exhausting. Even though it can be scary knowing rapids are along the way, when you surrender into the flow you can only be grateful when you make it through the rapids. In life, it can be scary to face challenges or obstacles; however, when you surrender, trust your intuition for guidance, and learn the lesson along the way, you will float through challenges with grace, only to feel gratitude looking back.

By the way, I have been white water rafting since that experience. Fear will only hold us back, unless we use it to push us through. Avoiding the rapids is only practicing resistance against the flow. Being in the flow of the river is the most joyous part. It is smooth, easy, and noticing the surroundings makes it magical.

It is no one else's responsibility to live your life. It is your responsibility. If you do not live your life, no one else will. You have a purpose, you have a dream and you have the capability to do anything and everything your heart desires. Look to the things that push your buttons as an opportunity to learn more about yourself, what you need to heal and what you need to learn. As you grow through your healing, you become a stronger you, with an unstoppable capability to share your gifts with others.

You are the Master Guru of your own life.

Eagle Exercise

Write a list of people in your life who push your buttons. Reflect on situations or experiences when those buttons were being pushed. What did you learn from those experiences? What can you learn about yourself from those experiences? What in that situation pushed your button? What do you think that is linked to? How did you respond in that moment? How can you respond differently to practice coming from a place of love?

THE FLIGHT

I always wanted to fly. In fact, I am still convinced that one day I will learn how to fly. I don't mean in a helicopter or in a plane. I mean just me, flying through the air. The desire is probably why I loved the movie Space Jam so much. First of all, I adored Michael Jordan growing up, but secondly, his dream was to fly. The theme song of that movie, 'I believe I Can Fly' resonates so well with me. In some of the greatest places I have visited, that song will come into my mind and I will sing it. These beautiful moments remind me of the infinite possibilities that exist. That is when the reminder that I believe I can fly trickles down to my heart. At times I will compare sitting on a chair to flying. When we sit down on a chair, we are so convinced, so trusting, that when we sit down that chair will hold us up. What if I convinced myself I could fly? What if I became so trusting and so certain that if I lift off I will soar? After all sitting in a chair is just an illusion I created with a set of beliefs. What if I created such a strong belief to fly and up I go? I feel it within me that I am mean to soar.

I heard a story once told by Bishop T.D. Jakes that changed me forever. I will share the story, with my own personal twist.

Chickens live their life with their head bobbing up and down, eating anything and everything at their feet. They will eat corn, stones, scraps, and shockingly, they will even eat their own feces. Yes, chickens eat a bunch of shit. Then people eat those chickens, but that's another story. Chickens live their life surrounded by other chickens that are all doing the same thing. They dig holes in the ground and they all cheer with a 'bock' when an egg is laid. They only eat what is at their feet because that is what they are looking at. They all stay together. If they are lucky, free-range chickens, they have a small area to roam around in. Yet, surprisingly, even if a chicken can go anywhere they wish to go, they never really wander far. Every once in a while a chicken might fly. Actually they jump, flapping their wings only to a height of four or five feet. They bob their head up and down and they wander around eating their own feces. They bock and they eat and they bock again. They might jump up, jump over or jump onto something, but, when a storm comes in, they all run into their chicken coop and hide away. This is a look at the life of a chicken.

The eagle, on the other hand, is at the top of the avian food chain. The eagle soars to the greatest of heights and powers through the air. The eagle sits patiently and calmly, overlooking the beautiful sights from the highest peaks. The eagle will swoop down effortlessly and grasp the best of the best to eat. Eagles are also strong swimmers, managing strong waters. When near water, they usually build their nests high and overlooking the coasts. They have excellent eyesight and are one of the only creatures that can stare directly into the sun without the blink of an eye. Eagles, spreading their wings with a wingspan of nine feet, soar through the sky with ease. When heavy winds challenge an eagle or a storm comes through, the eagle will face it head on and actually use the storm to fly to even greater heights. The eagle will fly right over the storm. If that is not fascinating enough, the male and female eagle will soar together and mate while flying through the sky. That is the look at the life of an eagle.

We can look to these two birds and learn quite a bit about who we are. Are we the chicken with our head down, bobbing and 'bocking' away, only looking to eat up our own crap over and over again, wondering why nothing ever changes? Do other chickens surround us in the same area, wandering around, eating their own crap over and over again and wondering why nothing ever changes? Are we running and hiding away when a storm comes through just to avoid getting wet? Or, are we the eagle that soars through the skies, seeing the beauty that surrounds us, looking to the sun without fear, feeding off the best of nutrients, using the storm and the winds only soar to greater heights and to fly above the challenge? Are we spreading our wings to their fullest potential and living a life of passion, living life along side others who will fly with us and mate with us in the sky?

I feel as though I was an eagle raised in a culture of chickens. I was told what to eat, how to eat, where to go, when to go, and how to go. People doing the same thing over and over and over again surrounded me. I saw people eat crap, digest it and then eat it again, wondering why nothing ever changed. I saw people try to fly. They got a few feet into the air, only to return again and dig a hole into the ground. I desired to fly and I knew I could, but what about all these chickens? Are they really chickens or are they just eagles raised in a chicken culture?

I was unhappy in the chicken coop. I was meant to fly to the highest of heights and soar through the sky. So, I began looking to the sun without a blink of an eye. I learned the direction to go and what I needed to eat to have the strength to get me there. I would take flight and use the storms only to fly higher. Then I would return to the chickens with different food and different stories. I would share about life outside of the chicken coop. I would speak with such passion and love that soon other chickens would want to try as well. That's when I knew, they weren't chickens; they were the eagles raised in a chicken culture. They started looking to the sun for direction and feeding off food other than their own crap and off they went. This is when my purpose was revealed.

The purpose of our life is linked to what brings us great passion. Passion empowers us to do what we are meant to do in our life. When we live without passion, we feel empty and lost. At some point, we all feel empty and lost. We all experience pain and challenges, but we must understand that the pain we experience leads us to our purpose. It is the pain that creates the desire to do what we are meant to do. When we push through the pain and grow from it, we can use the pain to drive us. We can use our manure to grow through it and not to carry it around or to eat it over and over again. Then we can share with others about how we have soared through challenges to be the person we are meant to be. We cannot find purpose and passion in life when we keep our head down only looking at our feet in front of us. We cannot find purpose and passion in our life if every time there is a storm we run and hide to avoid it. We must face the winds that challenge us head on and use those challenges to fly over the storm. What you might think is working against you is actually working for you.

If we stay in the chicken coop, we are not in the land of our dreams. We keep eating the same shit over and over again, wondering why nothing changes. Instead, we can begin to feed ourselves with something else. We can start to look outside of the coop to a world outside of everything that we have ever known. That does not have to be scary, it can be fun, exciting and empowering.

Finding your own purpose in life is your own responsibility. You have teachers to support you in becoming you. Teachers that come into your life to push buttons and to reveal the areas you need to heal, to grow and to learn. Some teachers teach what to do and others teach what not to do. Eagles can teach us tips in how to fly; chickens can teach us tips in how to jump. Know that everything you are and everything you wish to be is all part of the magic in finding your passion and living out your life purpose.

Surround yourself with people that are going to support your flight. Feed yourself with food that will give you strength. Physical food that keeps your physical body strong, but also mental food that will keep you focused on things that empower you. Uncover the tools to make things easier and guide you along your way. Everything you need you already have. Everything you need to know is right at your fingertips. We live in a time where more than 80 percent of all human knowledge can be found on the Internet. Use the Internet as a tool to empower you and to empower others, not as a tool to cause harm.

The Flight

Only one piece keeps an eagle flying and a chicken on the ground. That piece is what you eat. Notice what kind of knowledge you are absorbing to learn. Notice what kind of beliefs or truths you are adopting to be true. Notice the people who are feeding you. This is not an opportunity to judge other people. This is an opportunity to judge what you eat. It has nothing to do with everyone else around you and everything to do with you. It's not about noticing who are chickens and who are eagles while you sit back and observe. It is about noticing if you are the chicken or the eagle and learning what to feed yourself in order to fly if you so choose.

Ignite your purpose and your passion by igniting your mind and body. Feed your mind knowledge that will empower you. Feed your body food that will fuel you. Take care of your body. Your body is the most important tool you will ever have. When your body is not strong, you can only jump the four feet. Feed your mental-self empowering messages and learn how to feed your physical-self with powerful fuel. Diet is withholding something from your body. It is not about taking something away, it is about providing what is needed. All the chickens eat the same crap. Eat the most nutritious foods and learn exactly what the body needs to be in balance and to run at its fullest potential. When you drive a car, you put gas in the car in order for it to run. You do not drive endlessly or you'll find the car dead at the side of the road. You also do not fill the car with coca cola. You fill the car with the appropriate fuel. In addition, you get the oil checked, wash the car, vacuum the inside, check the fluids and you park the car. Learn to fuel yourself. Take care of yourself by providing yourself with the right fuel and fluids. And park! Take time to rest and to check in. Be the eagle and find the highest peak to overlook the greatest of sights and rest.

Some people may feel overwhelmed, wondering what their life purpose is. Don't get lost in confusion by focusing only on the destination. You might not know what your purpose is right in this moment and that's okay. Remember to enjoy the journey as you seek it out. Learn from the challenges and enjoy the beauty along the way. I felt overwhelmed for a very long time about what I was meant to do with my life. It still stuns me that they encourage children to be thinking about what they want to be when they grow up at a young age. I remember being in grade seven and having to answer questions about my career choice. I was thirteen years old! I had no idea what I wanted to be when I grew up! I struggled through high school as well, attempting to determine what I wanted to be when I grew up. Every year since childhood I changed. I wanted to be an actress, a model, a veterinarian, an astronaut, a talk show host, a writer, a teacher and each could change yearly, weekly or even daily. I had no idea. I loved so many things, I could not imagine choosing one. I remember being fifteen years old, spending what seemed like forever filling out a career questionnaire that was meant to reveal your best-suited career choices. After waiting impatiently for the program to calculate my answers, the best career choice that fit me perfectly ended up being a circus performer. I was so furious. It was that day I decided it's not what I am going to be, it is a matter of what I am going to do in this world! That was the day I decided I was going to spend my life doing a series of really cool things that made me happy. Later down my journey, it came to my attention that we are human beings not human doings and again my perspective expanded and I needed to take some time to ponder that. Our purpose is being. Who am I being?

We may not know our purpose right now or we may know exactly what our purpose is right now. It doesn't matter. It just matters who are you being right now. Are you being happy? Are you being fulfilled? Our purpose helps to generate a passion within us that fires up our light and gives us a reason to wake up before the alarm goes off; it gives us a skip in our step. Our purpose is created in our mind in connection with our heart. It is a matter of being as we seek the things we want to do in our life. Sometimes we need to be exactly where we are. This can even mean being in the middle of our manure. It can mean swimming in the cloudy water of rapids. Discover contentment in where you are. Notice where you are right now, honour that, love it and provide what you need to nurture yourself. Respond with love and compassion for just being you, where ever that is. Once you sit and notice where you are, you can begin to decide where you want to go. You begin a journey. Notice the things to be grateful for along the way, including the button pushers. You will learn lessons as you go and begin to grow through the manure. You will flourish, rooting into the earth of your manure, and opening up to the sun, growing fruits from your stems to share with others. As you shine your beauty, others will begin to appreciate your beauty too and enjoy in sharing the fruit from you to nourish from. The fruit you share likely has something to do with your purpose as you contribute and give back to others, overcoming all that you have grown through.

Choosing to uncover your purpose can happen at any given moment at any given age. It is simply a choice to be thirsty and to begin seeking it out. We do not need to know all the answers immediately. We just need to start asking the right questions to begin the adventure. It is setting your mind to something and taking flight towards it.

In short, it is the choice to fly.

Eagle Exercise

What are your greatest dreams and desires? What are the ideas and images you would picture and imagine when you were just a kid? What lights the fire in your heart that brings deep emotion of what you really feel strongly about? What brings you the most joy? Take a moment to answer these questions and to write a list of all the things in your life that make you the happiest. Look to your list and determine how often you take part in the things that make you happy. On the quest to uncover your passion and life's purpose, begin by focusing on doing things that bring you the most joy and happiness. That which brings you joy becomes the stepping-stones to living your purpose. Enjoy the journey.

THE TRAVELER

It is our birthright to be happy. We have been blessed to exist and what we do with that blessing is up to us, just us. Human existence has been plagued by negative events and by glorious ones, but throughout human existence one thing remains constant – each human being is responsible for his/her own self. You are responsible to intervene upon your own suffering. What will you do for yourself, for your peace, for your happiness?

We are on Earth at such a significant time in history. We have been able to connect to anywhere in the world, through traveling, through books, through the Internet, and can experience first hand different cultures to discover various perspectives and ways of thinking. We have seen people break records and achieve exceptional advancements. We can immediately connect with each other with a push of a button. People have walked grounds that were never dreamed of ever walking on. We know so much more about the Earth, the Universe and our abilities as humans, it is remarkable. We have the ability to step out of our day-to-day life and experience a world outside of what we ever thought possible.

The culture I was raised in really encouraged and valued education. The education system is believed to be a major tool in life. I spent ten years in an elementary school and four years in a secondary school, and I would not change any of my personal experience as it has led me to this moment. However, when I went to university I began to really understand that there was an entire world out there. I heard about it, but now I was beginning to realize it beckoned me. The desire to seek more, to soak up more, and to learn more created a fire within me. I realized what I needed to learn was not found in a textbook. It was not in the papers I was writing or the exams that would stress me out. What I needed was so much more than that. I will never regret my educational experience, as it was a stepping-stone to where I am today, struggles and all, but it was the burning to see the world that made me seek out more.

I wish I knew when I was younger that not everyone learned by reading and memorizing. Some people need to read and memorize, some need to discuss and talk it out, some people need to hear the information, and some people need to see it, touch it and be immersed within it. Everyone learns differently. Life is much easier when you can understand how you learn and apply that strategy to everything. When I was growing up I used to think there were only two types of people. Some people were told, 'do not touch the stove you will burn yourself.' They would trust that and not touch the stove. That would be enough. Other people were told the same, 'do not touch the stove you will burn yourself.' Those people needed to touch the stove and feel the burn in order to learn that when you touch the stove you burn yourself. Now I realize that there are also people who need to watch someone else burn him/herself. Others take apart the stove in order to understand how you can burn yourself, while some will just use the stove to cook and could care less about burning or not burning him/herself. These are just a few examples, but there are many. People learn in many ways. We can use many strategies to learn but, I must admit, some ways of learning can be much more enjoyable than others. Understanding how we learn can be a valuable asset to navigating life.

It was not enough for me to sit and to listen about how beautiful our world is. I needed to see it for myself. I needed to taste, touch, feel, smell and completely immerse myself in the world. I wanted to understand cultures, people and why things are the way they are. I wanted to explore how I could be part of making it a better place for all people. I realized that my little town of Bright's Grove, Ontario was a hidden gem and a beautiful place to grow up in, but it was not the only gem. I began to wander off. People thought I was lost, out in the world trying to find myself or trying to figure out my life. I believe it was the writer, J.R.R. Tolkien who said, "Not all who wander are lost." One could argue those who do not wander are the ones lost. In time I realized life wasn't about creating myself, it was about uncovering who I am and what my life was meant to be about. Once we understand who we are than we can really create the life we want to be in. We can create the life that is going to bring us the most joy and the most peace. It is a life that is lived with pure passion. Life is precious and it has the potential to be lived with bliss! I cannot comprehend why anyone would work a job that they hate, live in a home they cannot stand to be in, surround themselves with people who are miserable and hurtful, or live a life feeling dead. I don't get it? We need to wake the love up!

I may be perceived as a dreamer, but I am not the only one. Does this sound familiar? John Lennon certainly was not the only one. He knew a fulfilling, joyous life that began with a dream of what could be. It must begin as a dream. I am also not naive. I know people live in poverty and people struggle and face nasty experiences, I get it, but I also know that people who have come from those struggles have also come out of them. The difference is having an understanding that being stuck in a rapid is only a moment in time and eventually the river will continue to flow. It is called trust. Oprah Winfrey grew up in an abusive environment, hurt, degraded, and hopeless. Now she lives a life of abundance and strives to share with everyone how others can do the same. Walt Disney died before he could see his dream come true, but the truth is he saw it before anyone else did and began to make it happen. Michael Jordan didn't make the basketball team during his sophomore year in high school, but did he quit playing basketball? No, instead he trained even harder and pushed even harder because basketball was his passion. He was just some short kid from Brooklyn who made it happen. Justin Bieber was just a kid from a small town who loved to perform, so he made videos to post online. He did what he loved with passion and the right person noticed. He spent his time on his music, wishing to be a musician someday, but he didn't wait for someday, he was a musician every day, as the world now knows. We can choose to observe these people with a limiting belief that they are the lucky ones, but it has nothing to do with luck. It is about pushing through the pain and struggles and using them to overcome fear. It is about understanding who you are and sharing that with the people around you. Life is not just about you, when you live with love, abundance, joy, and peace, it radiates to all who surround you.

We do not necessarily need to go to a different country with a backpack to carry and wander aimlessly to really be a traveler. A traveler is someone who looks to the whole world with awe, noticing the beauty and the life upon it. A traveler is someone who seeks to master life. A traveler meets the desire to live life to the fullest, soaking up all there is to enjoy, and learning to live life not just be in a life. There is a distinct difference between a traveler and a tourist. A tourist stops in, takes some photos and says they have seen it all. A traveler stays a while, soaks up the moments and explores with curiosity. A traveler learns, reflects, is grateful and internalizes what is learned from each experience. A tourist demands, complains and judges. Travelers will immerse themselves in the culture, understand it and give something back with gratitude. Tourists leave a trail that others need to clean up. We may have had moments as the traveler and moments as the tourist, but the idea is to understand the difference and make a conscious decision which of the two you want to be.

The traveler is never alone. Sometimes that is what the traveler desires most- just to be alone. However, no matter where you go or what you do, someone or something is there to support you. Even in the depth of the woods, away from the rest of the world, creatures notice you are there, surrounding you and watching over you. We are never alone, only sometimes lonely. Lonely is a powerful place to be. It allows you the opportunity to learn who you are and to be comfortable in your own skin. You can understand what is held under the skin and explore all that you are and all you wish to be. Lonely is learning to be happy just being you. When you are who you are meant to be, you will never be lonely again because you love who you are. You love being around you. This is when 'alone' becomes an understanding that you are all one. You are whole just being you. See, being a traveler is not just about learning how to love the world around you; being a traveler is about learning how to love yourself. Peace begins within.

Lonely is one of many emotions that can reveal the world within our self. Many may believe that the only emotion we must try to achieve is to be happy or that happy is the only positive emotion. Happiness may include peace, joy, or excitement.   Feeling angry, frustrated, scared, lonely, or sad can all be considered negative emotions, but all emotions are part of being human. They are a beautiful part of being human. Our feelings reveal so much about who we are. It is so important to tune into the feelings that we are feeling, not only to explore what makes us happy, but also, what makes us angry or frustrated. What scares us most? What makes us sad? Usually exploring these questions will allow us to under-stand the root of our feelings. Why do we feel angry when someone cuts us off on the road? Why do we feel scared of heights? Why do we feel sad when a child is hurt?

We must learn to use our emotions as information about our self. Usually our emotions surface in certain situations. We look to the situation as the issue, but the situation is only the vessel to our emotions. Just as the spoon stirs up our cloudy water, our emotions are the salt that creates those clouds. When a situation occurs and generates a strong emotion, such as anger, sadness, or frustration, that emotion makes our water cloudy. This is usually an indicator that we have healing or learning to do. Our emotions are a natural part of us that unveil where we need healing and growth. Our emotions promote an opportunity for us to learn how to respond to those situations and not just react to them. We can take our time to think and to speak before responding. We can stop the urge to react with anger or frustration and instead respond from a place of love, love being the master of emotions. This may seem easy enough to consider, but it really does take practice and focus to achieve.

I am going to share an experience that was very difficult and at this time of writing this, happened quite recently. It is not an easy write and for some it may not be an easy read. However, with life we have to acknowledge the challenges and be transparent in order to understand, to learn and to grow. For that purpose, I feel this story can be shared. Out of respect to those who were directly affected by this experience I will not be using a real name.

On New Year's Day, January 1, 2013, I woke up a complete emotional mess. The night before I was with friends for dinner, but I ended up calling it an early night because I just wasn't feeling quite right. My stomach was in knots and I felt like I was going to be sick. I thought it was from the sushi or from the glass and a half of wine I had at dinner, but that wasn't the case. I was just feeling off, both emotionally and physically. The next morning it was even worse. I felt sad and then I felt angry. I went into a complete rage in my head about really, nothing. It was so bizarre. That afternoon I was meant to go to my grandparents' house for lunch and on my way there I decided I was too angry, I just couldn't be around anyone. I ended up going to my office, which thankfully holds such a healing space that I felt comfortable to be in. I layed on the floor in the fetal position and just cried. My thoughts were all over the map. As I was on the floor, in a total emotional mess, I started to be mindful of my thoughts and to become aware of what I was focusing on. I noticed that my thoughts were focused on being angry towards my parents for one single comment my mom said to me in the morning that was completely trivial. She mentioned that they were upset I didn't say Happy New Years to them the previous night, but she had no idea I wasn't feeling well. Normally it wouldn't have made a difference to me, but I was in such an emotional place, it became where I threw my rage. In my head I decided I was leaving town, disappearing from the world, etc, etc. As I began to become aware of what I was focusing on, it became more and more silly to me. I clearly didn't want to disappear and I actually adore my family. In fact, everyone was together, enjoying a great lunch and here I was crying on the floor of my office. That was not where I wanted to be, I was not in the emotion I wanted to be in and this was most definitely not how I wanted to spend my New Years Day. I moved my focus from things I was angry about to things I was thankful for. I was so grateful that my family spends time together in celebration and I was so grateful to have my whole family. We tend to forget how precious that is, and literally, I sat up, completely and totally fine. All my emotions completely settled and it was like a snap of the fingers, all was well. I know, bizarre. I know that where we focus we generate emotion and it was just a moment to practice it. Tony Robbins always states, energy flows where focus goes. Little did I know I was going to be challenged to master the power of focus and emotions.

Later that day, I was informed that a friend of mine had gone missing from the night before. I will name her 'Angel'. She was out with friends, had been drinking, got in a fight with her boyfriend, and left to go home. She left angry, and although others tried to stop her or talk to her, she left on her own and was missing since. Some of her closet friends and family were out searching for her all day. Soon the word got out and people in the whole city went out searching for her. Her family immediately started a Facebook group, which became the new local news hub. People posted on the group where they had searched or checked to see what areas still needed to be checked out. It all felt very unreal. People were searching for a couple of days, but finally the search was called off. A body of a girl in her twenties was found in a wooded area off a back road between towns. They called the search off, although they did not announce who was found. It became a waiting game. It felt like forever had gone by, in fact, I don't even recall the actual amount of time, by the end of the next day, or maybe it was two days, it's all a timeless fog. But, in the end, the police announced that it was her. She had been murdered.

We hear of these stories all the time if we watch the news enough. People go missing, people get murdered, and people experience tragedies. But this sort of thing just doesn't happen in Sarnia, Ontario Canada, and this sort of thing just doesn't happen to someone like Angel. Absolutely not. Angel was a year older than I am, but we attended the same elementary school and high school. She wasn't my best friend, but she wasn't an acquaintance either, she was just Angel! She was always a sweetheart, always hilarious, always passionate, always fun and always loving. She and I shared the same best friend so our paths crossed often. It didn't matter if it was one month or one year, Angel was just as welcoming, kind and funny. She was full of light and full of love and people like that don't get murdered. But, she did, and it was a very ugly situation. Within days the police arrested two people for her murder. Whether people knew Angel or not, the entire community was affected. The emotions that arose were an overload. People were in shock, people were angry, people were devastated, people were outraged, people were numb, people were fearful, people were shaken up and some people felt it all.

This experience was one shared by the entire community and beyond. I cannot speak for the thousands of people who were affected by this tragedy, I can only speak of my own experience and my own perspectives. Initially I think I was in shock. Soon I moved into a calm stillness, but it likely was still related to shock. A part of me still doesn't really believe it happened and another part of me is very aware that it happened. So many elements of this experience were close to home. Many people get drinking, get into an argument and leave angry. This happens to probably more than half a dozen people for every party. The reality that this could have happened to any one of us that has ever shared this experience became very real. A fortunate feeling moved in when I realized the number of times I walked off on my own, got mad at a boyfriend or left somewhere angry or upset. Angel was passionate; when she loved, she loved with her full heart and if she was mad, you knew she was mad. I've been mad, what happened to Angel could have happened to anyone, it could have happened to me numerous times. Perhaps a part of me even felt guilty for being so lucky to take mindless risks, usually to wake up the next day without a second thought about it. So many people would hop in a car for a ride home instead of pay for a cab, why not? I know I have accepted a ride home. I have travelled across the world and stayed with families who are complete strangers, of course I'd jump in to get a ride home. But why did this situation have to occur and why to Angel? What really happened that night? Who are those two people who were arrested? What did they do and more importantly why did they do it?

Nothing but empty questions arose and people came up with their own answers or attempted to find them. I quickly realized I had to practice mastering my focus. If I got on to Facebook and started reading people's angry comments of rage or depressing comments of personal relation to the whole situation, I noticed my emotions would follow. Suddenly everyone was a detective and everyone had a conviction. People were so angry. Of course I understand why people were angry, I get it, but the situation became a vessel for emotions to surface, I know it did for me. Although, I never felt angry like I noticed many others felt, and maybe a part of me feels guilty for that too, but I didn't have anger towards the two people who were arrested. I understand that many people believe too much evidence leads to their guilt; however, they still need to be proven guilty. Assuming they are guilty, I still can't manage to feel angry. If I take a moment to separate myself from having a relation to the beautiful being who was murdered, I am aware that the whole situation completely reflects the world we are living in. Those who murdered Angel come from a place with a complete lack of love, period. That is what darkness looks like. The need for love and acceptance is so high, that it develops the possibility of creating such a distorted reality of relationship and connection, for one to take, to attack, to torture, to rape, to beat, to kill and to murder. It doesn't matter what really happened that night, I don't need to know the real answers to know that it wasn't good; in fact, it's already a nightmare in my mind. I couldn't sleep for days. I didn't eat. I couldn't be left alone. I was fine during the day, but at night, nothing but fear arose. I was disoriented, moving through motions of a situation I couldn't make sense of. I would leave my office and walk to my car, a walk I do hundreds of times, and suddenly I was on edge, looking over my shoulder, heightened awareness to every sound and to every movement. My body would shake, I'd lose my sense of breath and there I was, in a place of fear. I understand that fear serves a purpose, it's a defense mechanism, but I know it is not mentally, emotionally or spiritually healthy to be sitting in that place all the time. My consciousness was trying to deceiver the moments I was safe and the moments I wasn't. I'm sure Angel wasn't walking in fear. She was moving forward boldly, fiercely, likely with enough emotion to break through a wall, but that obviously didn't matter.

This experience surfaced the emotions that I needed to release, that may have been stored in pockets I buried away somewhere. I allowed those emotions to surface, I noticed them, I felt them and I figured out a way to move through them; this is how I mastered focus in relation to emotions. Even though our emotions give us an opportunity to see where we need healing and growth, we can use those emotions to move through as slowly or as quickly as we choose. We are always choosing. When I would get on Facebook and read everyone else's pain, misery and reflections, I would find myself sink. I did not want to focus on the anger, the rage or the fear. None of that reflected Angel and at the end of the whole experience, it didn't matter what happened, who did it or how, a beautiful, loving, star on earth died. That girl had a name, a face, an identity and a legacy that was getting lost in the darkness of a situation and that's what I began to focus on, the light. In this case, it was easy. Angel was the light.

I started to focus on the person Angel was; a young adult who had already made a massive difference in so many people's lives. She was a kindergarten teacher and she would bring in lunches, footwear, clothing or supplies for students who did not have those things. This may seem like her simple contribution; however, someone decided to start a fundraiser called Angel's Gift where people could donate money that would go towards providing school supplies and necessities to children who did not have them. Within the week thousands of dollars was raised for Angel's Gift and now, I'm sure it's well over $50,000. This alone is a reflection of Angel and her love towards others through her life. Another group organized a balloon release that gathered family, friends and community members together to recognize a difficult event and to release part of the burden collectively through a symbolic gesture. Another group organized a candlelight vigil and hundreds of people gathered together at a time of darkness to light candles, to honour Angel and to generate thoughts and prayers for her friends, family and to those hurting. Months have gone by and people continue to offer various gestures or acts of kindness to reflect the kind of person Angel was and the type of life that she lived. She set an example for people to see what light and love can look like. By witnessing her beautiful example, others can choose to radiate that same light and love. These things don't bring Angel back or take away what happened to Angel, but by focusing on the powerful, light-filled gestures the suffering of a painful event can subside.

I had moments I questioned the safety of my home city, moments of questioning even if the world was a safe place to be. I felt fearful, abused, shaky, numb, guilty and most definitely, I felt devastated. In that whirl of emotions, I took time to sit with each one. In fact, there were times I just sat and did nothing but stare and feel completely numb. I also attempted to move through the motions of life. Going back to work was brutal. I tried to focus on things that required my attention and energy and it was next to impossible. At one point I decided to photocopy papers I needed for a group three months away that needed to get done, eventually, but really it was just a mindless activity that I could do to feel I was being productive. A co-worker walked in, gave me a hug and expressed how she had been thinking of me as everything was going on. It was a very kind gesture, but it was the moment that made the whole experience become real. I had a meltdown, crying and could barely breathe. I had to sit out for a bit and just bring my focus to my breath and push out all of the emotions that I didn't realize I was storing. I practiced much more yoga and meditation than usual, just to move out the emotions and not store them in my body. I practiced every single breathing technique I have ever learned or taught in order to release all that surfaced through the experience. Really, the whole experience provided a deep healing of old and fresh wounds. I wish everyone who was impacted by this experience could understand how a horrific event can provide the opportunity to surface stored emotions and release them to heal on so many levels. Consciously or subconsciously everyone recognized that Angel was really one of us and we instantly were forced to face mortality. Many parts of who we are could identify with this experience and it made a massive and deep impact for many people. It provided an opportunity to unleash emotions we normally suppress, what a gift, what healing. Even though it felt like parts of it took forever to get through, it really is a blessing that the overall experience happened quickly. She was found, which allowed everyone to have ease knowing that. Two people were arrested for her murder and there is ease in knowing that as well. These types of things are hidden gifts in a dark situation. The whole experience was a difficult one that provided many lessons to learn and an opportunity to respond with love and not fear. The souls involved in this event created the space for this healing, learning and growth to occur, not just Angel, but also her murders.

I refuse to think that my home city is an unsafe place to be and I refuse to think that our world is an unsafe place to be. Yes, bad things happen all over the map, but every bad thing that occurs generates more good to occur in ripples. If we only see the darkness and negative incidents we are neglecting the powerful movements, growth, awareness and events that come from those incidents. This is on a mass level, but more importantly, this is on a personal level in each and every life. We are constantly choosing our thoughts, our words and our actions that reflect either love or fear. This experience put me to the challenge, but even through that, focusing on the love is what allowed me to grow, learn lessons and to offer a support to others through a difficult time. My lessons of love have been shared with others to offer another perspective on how to cope in life; however, those lessons have also been learned and practiced in order to help me cope in my own life. I recognize the tough world we are living in and it has its shadows, as we all do, but responding with love is the light that becomes the contrast to those shadows. We can be the change we wish to see in the world and we can be the love we wish to feel in the world.

More often than not, people look to others for love or to the outside world to receive love. However, when we provide self-love we choose to respond to the world around us from a place of love. This ability will in fact fill us with all of the love that we need. When we are full, then we can turn to others to share that love. We must learn to not only speak to others with compassion, love and understanding, but also to speak to our self and about our self with that same compassion, love and understanding. What kind of conversation are we having in our head? Do we berate or criticize ourselves? Again, do we tell our self how ugly, stupid and fat we are? Does that really reflect self-love? When we speak to our self with love and provide messages of strength, support, love, and empowerment, we feel full and whole. Self-love is similar to the love we give to others and we provide understanding, compassion, presence, joy, and freedom. We do not need to seek that feeling from anything or anyone outside of us. We provide for the self, we are full, happy, joyful, and peaceful. When we are full, then we have the love, patience and energy to provide the same for others. Again our thoughts and words can be used for empowerment and we can start within.

This can be difficult to do. If we spent our whole life till now thinking and speaking negatively in our mind and through our words, this can potentially be a challenge. Unfortunately we live in a society where we are programmed to feel like we are never enough, never good enough, never smart enough, and eventually we begin to believe these lies. Some of us are raised in a home where we are told we are not enough. If up until now this has been your experience, telling yourself that you are awesome, amazing, sexy, fun, loving and playful may really start to feel

---

silly. That's okay. Be silly. Give yourself permission to be a kid again. Being a traveler is a bit like being a kid. You explore the world with that same wonderment and curiosity. Everything is new and rich. Life is playful and exciting. We can do this in our every day journey. We can do this within our self. When we feel angry and frustrated about something insignificant, just notice. Reflect on where those feelings are coming from. Be gentle with yourself. Begin to practice being mindful in how you respond to the world rather than reacting. This will break old habits and old ways of thinking. At times you slip up, that's okay. Be gentle with yourself and then fix it. Know that as long as you are alive you have time to fix it. Take ownership when you make a mistake. Be humble, learn to apologize and above all, learn to forgive. Forgive those who have made mistakes and also forgive yourself for the mistakes you have made. We are all human and it happens. But own it and then do it differently. We do not need to repeat mistakes, but we most definitely can learn from them. Creating a different way of thinking and being takes commitment, practice and conditioning.

When you go to the gym to work out, you don't just walk in and pick up the heaviest weights. You start light and work yourself up. You build the muscles in your body. Becoming strong and fit doesn't mean you have the freedom to stop working out. You simply do what you need to do to maintain that strength and fitness level. You continue working those muscles. Becoming emotionally fit works in the same way. You start by noticing your emotions. Then you begin to reflect on where the emotions are coming from. You develop a better understanding of yourself and notice what your limiting beliefs are and where they came from. Then you take time to replace them with empowering thoughts and words. This is really developing new neuropaths in your brain and it takes time to strengthen them. You can start to be the person you desire to be right now. You work on your happy muscles. You condition your happiness and then you continue to do what you need to do to maintain it. For me, practicing yoga, meditation, spending time on my own in nature or listening to empowering music can all support this practice. At this point, you work on responding from a place of love. You may feel as though you master how to love yourself, how to love others and how to respond to the world around you with love. This doesn't give you the freedom to just stop. Other emotions might come up for you and that is okay. You work through them by sitting in that emotion, understanding it and using your power of focus to move through it. You begin to learn how to use your emotions to drive you. Use anger, frustration and fear to push you forward instead of holding you back. Use happiness, joy, peace, love and freedom to move towards and become more a part of it. Once you begin to understand yourself, have fun, be silly, and enjoy the journey. Learn to laugh with yourself. Humour is magic. But above all, be grateful.

Eventually you will begin to understand that your emotions are in direct relation to what you are focusing on. If you are focusing on things that irritate you, upset you or piss you off, well then you can bet that you will feel angry and frustrated. If you are focusing on things that disappoint you, make you sad or hurt you, then you can bet you will feel sad and upset. This may seem pretty basic, however, in the midst of a situation, you really need to be extremely mindful of where your thoughts are and what you are focusing on. Every situation creates a sky of fireworks. You can be focusing on the different colours and which colours you like or don't like or you could be focused on which shape of firework you like best. You could focus on the fact that millions of dollars were spent on those fireworks and what a waste of money it is or you could be focused on looking at something spectacular with the person you love standing next to you. Your head might even be focused on all the things you have to do after the fireworks. Or perhaps, what you didn't do before the fireworks. Reflect on the different things that you could be focusing on. There is no right or wrong; however, depending on what you focus on, will definitely generate a different feeling of emotion. The question is, what emotion do you want to be in? For me, love is the master emotion that I always want to be in. That doesn't mean I am always in it. When other emotions arise, I honour those emotions and work to returning to that space of love again.

Traveling has the potential to teach one how to master living. When you can look at your day with the eyes of a traveler, exploring the world around you with wonder and curiosity, then you have mastered living. When you can sit and eat every meal, enjoy every bite, notice every taste bud kicking in, every flavour, and every texture, then you have mastered living. When you can spend time with the people in your life, nourishing these relationships and really listening and engaging in conversations to really get to know those people with sincerity, then you have mastered living. When you spend time every day to be alone to think, to reflect and to notice your feelings and your needs in the moment that you are in, then you have mastered living. When you notice each tree, flower and plant, acknowledge the bugs, birds and animals around you, recognize the sun when it rises and sets, acknowledge the moon and the stars in the sky at night, then you have mastered living. When each day includes all of this and you open and close your eyes, feel every feeling, acknowledge every breath, honour your body, honour your being and give thanks for it all, this is when you have mastered living. Paradise surrounds us every day no matter who we are or where we are. We just have to see it, acknowledge it and be grateful. When a traveler can take what they have learned during the travels and apply it to every day life, then the traveler has mastered living.

It is your birthright to master living your life and it is your choice to choose love.

Eagle Exercise

Take time to learn how you learn and develop a thrill and desire to learn more. Take five minutes to sit alone in silence and just notice how you feel in this moment. Notice how you physically feel and notice how you emotionally feel. Just notice. Bring your focus to your breath and focus only on your breath. As a thought comes into your mind, notice without judging and then bring your focus back to your breath. Learn to check in with yourself like this daily. You will learn what your mind, body and spirit needs and then you can choose to provide it.

THE RETURN HOME

The first time I traveled on my own, I learned so much about the world and about myself. I lived in Australia for a year. I traveled the country and dipped into parts of Asia and Fiji. It was a remarkable milestone of my life. I felt as though every part of me changed. When I returned home, I found it very difficult to merge back into the life I was living before I left. I found that people were interested in my trip and wanted to know how it was, yet realized those people weren't really that interested. People were interested to hear that the trip was good and they were interested in maybe one or two highlights but that was it. At first I was offended by this disinterest because I felt like there was so much to share. I thought it was worth their time and attention to hear about it. But I didn't receive that time and attention, after all it would have taken another whole year! Instead they wanted to share with me what was going on in their life. It took a couple of trips away and returning again to realize this was just the way it was going to be. People didn't really care all that much. The truth is they cared to know that things went well and that I was good. My safety and happiness was all that was important to them and I appreciate that. The traveling was not for those people; the traveling was for me. It was what I needed to do to uncover me. It was what I needed to do to understand life, where I fit into it and how I could create an even better life for myself. It was what I needed to do in order to understand the world. Traveling had everything to do with returning home.

Returning home was about returning home within myself. I am what I was traveling for. I am what I was seeking. I am what was under all that pain, confusion, experiences, and manure. I am a traveler so that I could return to me. I am the home. Understanding the return home is being in a place of peace, a place of love and a place of comfort. My home is sacred and precious. It is worth uncovering and it is worth keeping clean and tidy. It is worth every challenge and difficult experience because every stepping-stone surrounds the temple. The temple is the divine. Being one with the divine is being in a place of love and a place of peace. It is home to all of us.

Life is what we choose to make it. We can be our own role model. My entire soul not only craves to live a life of peace, my soul craves a world of peace. I would always read about beings of the past that radiated peace and learned about them with awe. I adored Mother Teresa, Mohandas Gandhi, John Lennon, Jesus Christ, Martin Luther King Jr., Rosa Parks, Dalai Lama, Margaret Mead, Siddhartha Gautama, and Nelson Mandela. Anyone who stood for change towards peace and love for all was someone I wanted to stand with. These are the people I look up to. They are not the lucky ones. They are just people who modeled what they wanted in life. They are people who modeled what they believed and what they stood for. They are people who modeled what is possible.

When we return home, it is not about bombarding people with our stories and experiences and making everyone see it our way. When we return home, it is about modeling who we have become and sharing love, compassion, understanding and joy. People learn in many different ways. Some people want to hear about it. Some people need to see it. Some people need to touch, taste and experience it. Some people need to do it their own way. Returning home with love and peace is about sharing it with others. When you are full of love, it is infinite and we do not run out. We do not need to give it in doses. We do not need to give it only when we receive it. We give and we give and we give with an open heart, an open mind and open arms for hugs! Love is the essence of being fully alive. Every single person on the planet desires to feel love and fears not being good enough. It does not matter the language, the culture, the gender or the age. That is our genetic, cellular, energetic being. This is why love is a universal language.

Love must be cherished and nurtured. When we return home, we have to care for that home. We must understand our mind, body and spirit as a whole and understand what we need to do as an individual to nurture who we are, consistently and constantly. It can be different strategies for everyone, but it has to be something, because nothing comes from nothing. Taking care of the body and learning to quiet the mind and connect with the spirit allows love to flow fluidly, gracefully, fully. You may not understand what love looks like in this moment, depending on what luggage you hold or if you are still an eagle in a chicken coop, and that is okay. Just know that it exists and be open to receiving it. What you seek you shall find. Hold the desire to be full of love and not full of shit!

Every movie has a main character looking to go after something or someone. The character wants to accomplish something or the character is in love with someone and wants to be with that person. The movie is filled with obstacles and challenges and in the end the character conquers. Perhaps the character doesn't get what he/she was after during the whole movie, but then it ends with a lesson or moral. This is our life. We are living the movie script; we are living the storybook. We are the main character. We spend time entertained by other characters, but it is time to become our own character and create the story we want to write. What are we after? I will save you time and tell you right now, we are all seeking love and we all fear something. We are solely responsible for successfully discovering what we are seeking in life, just as we are solely responsible for holding our self back or becoming our own barrier.

You are worth exploring. When you clean out your home and fill it with all that you love, it becomes a beautiful palace to dwell in. You are your home. Once your home is clean and filled, then you can contribute supporting others to organize, de-clutter and decorate their home with love as well.

That's really what this book is all about. It is a journey of a Monkette, who uncovered love, peace and joy. It was bliss, but the only thing missing was more people to enjoy the bliss with. I thought it was my job to get everyone there, but it wasn't. As it turns out, I got my own journey to travel and you have yours. It's not about carrying people along it's about walking with them. So I'm strolling, enjoying the beauty, and looking forward to have you to walk with. At the end of the day the answer to any question is love. How can you live love, how can you be love, how can you respond with love, and how can we share love with the world to be the generation that is world peace? I can tell you it's possible because I have grown through struggles and challenges and I have soared in the lights of the universe. Challenges still arise, but they are nothing but a moment in time and an opportunity to master love again. I get confused, frustrated, impatient, but then I sit with it and smile. Life is really what we are choosing to make it. Our belief systems, our thoughts and our words are creating the reality around us right now, in this moment. If you don't like your reality, change your thoughts about it. Let me just fill you in, the world around you is so much larger than you think it is. It's greater than your imagination, greater than what humans have ever known or explored. If you are surrounding yourself in a world that is suffering, may you be guided to wake the love up and step out of your reality and into a place of bliss. That is where I will meet you!

It is your human birthright to be happy, start there. Figure out what makes you happy and do more of it. Figure out what makes you unhappy and do less of it or change it for you and for everyone. Take time to get to know who you are. Understand that relationships are invisible mirrors. When you point a finger at someone, you have three more fingers pointing back at you. What are you projecting onto others that should be explored about yourself? What ignites your emotions is usually going to lead you to your passion or to the healing of your pain. Life is a sacred privilege that is a gift for you. How you choose to live your life is your gift back to the world and to yourself. Allow yourself to dream and then live those dreams while you are awake in reality. Remember it is not just about you. Your joy, love and happiness ripple through to everyone around you and throughout the world for all. The choices you make are your responsibility and within your control. These choices determine your life. What you choose to think, to speak and to do creates who you are. You are making these decisions every single moment. No one else is making these decisions for you. Be mindful of each moment. You can choose the life you want to live and you can choose to live a great life! Imagine it in your mind and step into your life. You are already home, you just have to open the door to passion and fill the rooms with love.

Welcome to your life. How are you going to live it?

Eagle Exercise

Do something right now, in this moment that is a step into a life that you love. Give yourself a gift of self-nurture or complete something that you have always wanted to do. Do something right now, in this moment that you love and that brings you joy. It's a celebration, you just completed reading the first book that made our paths cross in your journey!

YOU CAN LIVE AND LOVE WITH LAURA!

Take action in your own life!

Be the change you wish to see in the world.

Be the love you wish to feel in this world!

Join our community for love and support!

Join us on Facebook!
Be part of the ripple of love and LIKE our page:
www.facebook.com/liveandlovewithlaura

Check out classes, seminars or individual sessions
to discover you with Laura:
www.lauralouise.ca

Subscribe to weekly episodes of Live & Love With Laura:
www.youtube.com/liveandlovewithlaura

Learn more about this book and receive free videos at:
www.discoveryoubook.com

Thanks for being part of the journey.
Much love and safe travels!

Laura Louise

Manufactured by Amazon.ca
Bolton, ON

38935525R00072